MY LIFE AS A
single mom

Seven Biblical Lessons
for Transforming Your Life and Family

DR. O'SHEA LOWERY

innovo PUBLISHING

Published by Innovo Publishing, LLC
www.innovopublishing.com
1-888-546-2111

innovo
PUBLISHING

Providing Full-Service Publishing Services for Christian Authors, Artists & Ministries: Books, eBooks, Audiobooks, Music, Screenplays, Film & Curricula

My Life as a Single Mom
Seven Biblical Lessons for Transforming Your Life and Family

Book 1
THE STRONG & COURAGEOUS SINGLE MOMS SERIES

Library of Congress Control Number: 2022944766
ISBN: 978-1-61314-791-7

Cover Design & Interior Layout: Innovo Publishing, LLC

Printed in the United States of America
U.S. Printing History
First Edition: 2022

Has God called you to create a Christian book, eBook, audiobook, music album, screenplay, film, or curricula? If so, visit the ChristianPublishingPortal.com to learn how to accomplish your calling with excellence. Learn to do everything yourself or hire trusted Christian Experts from our Marketplace to help.

christian
PUBLISHING PORTAL

Dedication

I want to dedicate My Life as a Single Mom *to my two children, Randy Lowery and Mandy Morrow. My children were never afforded the opportunity to have a dad in their lives, as they were in their toddler years when their father died. I can't imagine how hard it was on them at times not to have this blessing. Yet never did they complain about the matter.*

I am so proud of both of my children. Today, Randy and Mandy have families of their own, occupations they enjoy, and churches they faithfully attend. They have stood by me, loved me, and loved one another throughout the years. I am so proud that God gave to me Randy and Mandy. I am so proud to be called their mom.

Contents

foreword

I am a "knower." Whisperings from the Holy Spirit seldom come to my inner ear, so when I heard *this is your chance* on that late spring Sunday morning, I listened. It was announced that our church was starting a single moms Sunday school and ministry, and the Spirit reminded me of a long-ago promise—a promise I made to God while I was single, that if I should ever marry, I would not forget singles and their pursuit of God's call on their lives.

You see, the world is very "married," very coupled up. This is never more real than when you are single. Singles are so busy doing life all by themselves, so you might think they have no one else to please, to discuss or argue with. But a single person also has no one to share the load and burden with. This makes single life different . . . harder in some ways. Single moms are overwhelmingly busy and burdened and sometimes burned out.

Shea Lowery has lived the single mom life since she found herself thrust into widowhood the morning of her husband's unexpected death. As a mom of two toddlers and with no college education or job, she looked into the mirror of that hospital room and cried out to God, asking, *What should I do?* God has been answering that question for nearly forty years now. With three college degrees including a doctorate, two successful children with good marriages and homes, and precious grandchildren, Shea has lifelong experience learning to wait on God and move only at His command. She is disciplined and determined, and she's a willing student of His.

Dr. Lowery continues to be about His work of drawing single moms into God's presence in practical ways, which she is uniquely able to do. She's the real deal. Sparkling southern vernacular and all!

God stands at the end of history. He knows the outcome of your life and of your children. He yearns to help be a part of your struggles, joys, and sorrows. He wants to help you raise your kids . . . plain and simple. Here. Now. Today.

God is aware of your unmet needs, and He's particularly sensitive to you because you hold the future of your own babies in your hands. God knows this, and He cares. It's clear in the scripture, both old and new, that the woman, the mother, ultimately bears the burden of her children's earthly futures and their eternal futures. That's why, as women, He comes to us where we are. You are the provider, educator, and decision maker, and God cares about you and your daily decisions. He's always been there and will always be there because His character never changes. It is who He is.

We hope your participation in this Bible study, written just for you, will bless your life, relieve your anxieties, and help usher you and your children and your children's children through the gates of heaven someday, generation after generation to come! God bless you as you learn.

—Charla and Paul Vinyard
Chairman of the Board (& Board Member) for Entrusted Hope Ministries, Frisco, Texas

Introduction

I t was April 27, 1990, a day forever engraved in my mind. As the sun came up on this particular morning, no one could have envisioned what awaited a twenty-four-year-old mom and her children, and no one could have imagined the sorrow that would overshadow their hearts.

My husband awoke for work as was his normal routine. Jeff was a construction worker, and he enjoyed his occupation quite well. The drive for him each day was close to an hour. Therefore, he arose early to get to work by daybreak.

Later in the morning, the kids and I awoke and began to prepare for the day. My home church was having a revival during this particular week, and on this exact evening, it was scheduled to be friendship night. I was looking forward to visiting people to invite them to church, so the kids and I gathered our things and proceeded toward the mission.

Back in those days, we had no cell phones, so inviting people to a church function required either calling on a home extension or showing up at someone's door. However, as the day progressed, with my children in tow, I suddenly developed a sick headache. I attempted to stay the course for a time, but the throbbing persisted. Unable to continue, I drove to my sister's home to visit and to rest. Yet, unknown to me, I was about to have a visitation of my own.

Shortly after arriving at my sister's home, the phone rang with my mother on the other end. "Keep her there," was the message conveyed. "We are on our way." No words were uttered to me that an accident had happened, nor did my sister tell me who was on the phone. We just continued to talk and to visit.

A little while later, my mother arrived, walking swiftly through the door to my sister's home. As she quickly helped gather my things, she calmly explained that my husband had been in an accident. Little information was given as I climbed into her car and headed to the hospital.

As we proceeded down the drive, my mind was engulfed with questions as to what had transpired. I wondered if Jeff was OK and even what he might be going through. While nervously anticipating the arrival, I continued to grapple with the unknown.

Finally, after arriving at our destination, I was told where to go for information. When I reached the specific floor of the hospital, I ran up to the desk to inquire about my husband. Yet, as I turned to witness a doctor speaking with my mother, I noticed a distraught look come over her face. I knew immediately that something bad had happened.

As I walked over in the direction of the doctor, I was slowly led into a separate room. The doctor had me sit down in one chair, while he sat in another one across from me. Unable to fathom what I was about to hear, I sat quietly and waited. As the physician began to speak, I honestly do not remember every word he uttered, but I do recall the news he delivered. My husband had been electrocuted and killed instantly at his job site. With those words, I immediately fell to pieces.

By this time, additional family members began to arrive. My mother was by my side with my aunt on her knees in front of me, ministering as best they could. Both my daddy and sister had walked through the door with my two babies. Yet, all I wanted to do was to see my husband.

While I waited, I continued to receive information about what had happened to Jeff. As details emerged, I remained in my chair with my head bowed and tears flowing. Then, after a period of communication, I was given permission to enter the room where he lay.

As I headed down the hallway toward the cubicle that housed my spouse, I was led by my mother. I arrived at the door's entrance where my husband was, and fear suddenly overtook me. In the process of moving slowly toward him, I began to tremble greatly. I could not believe what had transpired over the course of a few hours. My heart was breaking with emotions in disarray.

Finally, after reaching his side, I collapsed on his body, weeping profusely. I did not want to let him go. Jeff and I were only a few days away from celebrating our fourth anniversary. Yet, instead of making preparations for such a time, I would now be planning his funeral.

After a period of time with my husband, it was now time to say goodbye. As I returned down the hallway that had led me to Jeff, I veered into a restroom and found myself gazing intently into a mirror hanging over the bathroom sink. As I pondered all that had transpired, I cried out, *Lord, what am I going to do?* I was a stay-at-home mom with no college education; the next step would be uncertain, to say the least.

Yet even though calamity had come to my family, God's faithfulness would not be altered, nor even compromised. A new journey had been ordained, and through His grace, God would bring my children and me to the other side of tragedy, entrusting us with lessons we would never forget. God took a mess and made a message, while birthing a ministry entitled *Strong and Courageous*.

How to Use This Book:

My Life as a Single Mom: Seven Biblical Lessons for Transforming Your Life and Family is composed of collective wisdom from God's Word as it relates to a single mom's journey in life. The information is grouped into seven lessons that are essential for single moms to understand and put into practice in their daily lives.

Each week, you will study and discuss one of the seven lessons presented in the book. Brief reading assignments and written responses to questions are required for 5 of the 7 days in each weekly lesson. The day's assignments are then reviewed as a group or with the instructor.

Through His Word, God has given us principles to instruct us, wisdom to guide us, and truths to stand on as we travel forward as single moms. When you finish this course, you will have developed a better understanding of our biblical call to (1) Follow God all Our Lives, (2) Persevere and Stay the Course, (3) Be Courageous, (4) Wait On the Lord for Wisdom and Direction, (5) Remember God's Faithfulness, (6) Trust God Completely & (7) Obey God Completely.

Week 1

The Call to follow

~*Check with your instructor about when to view this week's video.*

During Week 1, we will address the following subject matters, focusing on biblical truths which give direction to our lives:

Day 1: "God Calls—We Follow" focuses on single moms who will be taught biblical truths with regard to the Lord's call. Ladies will be instructed that God is the One who calls, and their role is simply to pray, listen, obey, and follow.

Day 2: "Our Egypt" discusses truths which will be imparted to mothers about the importance of advancing in their journeys instead of retreating when faced with difficulties.

Day 3: "Returning to Our First Love" highlights how single moms will be taught to return to Jesus should they ever find themselves drifting from their intimacy with God due to the busyness of life, embracing a prodigal lifestyle, and so forth.

Day 4: "An Eternal Perspective on Conflicts" will teach the ladies in brief biblical truths how to relate to conflicts and how to handle them biblically.

Day 5: "Walking on Our Inheritance" will help single moms reflect once more on previous certainties taught throughout the week while being challenged to arise and walk with God in His foundational promises for their lives.

Day 1: God Calls—We Follow

I was riding home from college one day when the Lord brought to mind a particular church in Northwest Alabama. Uncertain as to God's reasoning behind such an impression, I reflected on that ministry for the remainder of the trip. Surprisingly my heart was being drawn to a church I knew nothing about.

After arriving at home, I made some phone calls to inquire about the congregation God had placed upon my heart. To my dismay, I was told the doors of the church were about to close. In fact, a total of fourteen people had decided it was time to dissolve the church because of the congregation's decline.

Weeks later, I found myself sitting in a room at a home, listening to a member describe the many prayers offered to God on behalf of the congregation. The woman stated, "Shea, we were praying on this side of the county for God to send help. As you were coming home from a long distance, He spoke to you about our need, and here you are." Clearly God was intervening on behalf of His Church while calling out various individuals to join Him. What appeared to be a hopeless situation was about to turn into an unforgettable journey of rebuilding.

Over time, more people started attending worship and serving in areas of leadership. New classes were started as well as choirs for both youth and adults. Finally, the day came when a pastor was called to lead the church. God was truly at work in the hearts of His congregation, and He was certainly at work within mine. While serving His people in this place, God called me to the ministry. I answered His leading to be in full-time Christian service and made my calling public while standing before the small congregation. This call was an unforeseen outcome of my earlier obedience, an outcome I never saw coming.

Nothing is more humbling than being called by God. A sense of amazement overwhelms the heart of the one called, for God has chosen him or her to carry out His will. This opportunity to follow a loving Savior elicits joy as well. Throughout God's Word, we read of countless individuals who received an invitation to follow God and join Him in His work. Some struggled with the call, while others immediately obeyed. Take a few moments to read about the calls of Amos, Jeremiah, and Jesus' earliest disciples.

Amos's Example: Amos 7:14-15

Then Amos replied to Amaziah, "I am not a prophet, nor am I the son of a prophet; for I am a herdsman and a grower of sycamore figs. But the LORD took me from following the flock and the LORD said to me, 'Go prophesy to My people Israel.'"

According to verse 14, what was Amos' trade?

What did the Lord take Amos from and what did He call him to do?

Jeremiah's Example: Jeremiah 1:4-10

According to verse 5, when did God call Jeremiah?

What did the Lord appoint Jeremiah to do? Did he respond to God's call in fear or in faith?

According to verses 7–8, what encouragement did God give Jeremiah in regard to his uncertainty?

According to verse 9, how did God equip Jeremiah for the task He had called him to?

Peter and Andrew's Example: Matthew 4:18-22

What work did Peter and Andrew do when they received the call from Jesus to follow Him?

How did both men respond?

Notice verse 19: "And He said to them, 'Follow Me, and I will make you fishers of men.'" Go back and circle the invitation, "Follow Me." Next, underline the promise, "I will make you fishers of men." Jesus' call to Peter and Andrew was first to *follow Him*. They never had to concern themselves over where they would be going, for Jesus already had their direction mapped out and their voyage set. They were first and foremost called to follow. Second, Jesus assured both men that *He* would *make them* "fishers of men."

An important truth to remember in regard to one's calling: Jesus is the One who equips His children for Kingdom building; through His Word, His Spirit and by various other means. What a relief to know that whenever God calls us to undertake a task, He equips us for that task.

How did James and John respond to the call of Jesus?

A calling always precedes a journey. This calling directs God's children to the path which He has already ordained for them. Unique and yet at times difficult, these routes are always aligned with God's unique purpose for each individual life. In addition, the obedient walking of these paths will always require death to self and surrender to Christ.

Thousands of years ago, God placed a special calling on a man to embark upon a voyage that would entail moments of victory, failure, and blessings. Join me as we examine Abram's call as well as his God-appointed journey.

Read Genesis 12:1-4.

> **Look once more at Genesis 12:1. Where did God call Abram from?**
>
>
> **What information did God give Abram with regard to where He was leading him?**
>
>
> **List all the promises God made to Abram in verses 2–3.**
>
>
> **Reread verse 4a: "So Abram went forth as the LORD had spoken to him; and Lot went with him." According to this passage of scripture, how did Abram "go forth"?**

Even though Abram did not possess all the facts, he moved forward—not by sight but by faith in God's character and His spoken Word.

> **How old was Abram when God called him to this new journey?**

Read Genesis 12:5-9.

> **What was the name of Abram's wife?**
>
>
> **According to verse 7, how did the Lord encourage Abram?**

Reread Genesis 12:8:

> **Then he proceeded from there to the mountain on the east of Bethel, and pitched his tent, with Bethel on the west and Ai on the east; and there he built an altar to the LORD and called upon the name of the LORD.**

> **According to verse 8, what three important actions did Abram take?**

Abram was residing in the land of promise. He had settled in, built an altar to God, and entered into a time of prayer and worship. He was thankful for his journey, in love with the One who ordained it, and in awe of the promises made to him.

In closing, I want us to recall several important factors about Abram's calling and journey while prayerfully applying these truths to our own journey.

1. It was God who called Abram to a particular path, not Abram who called God to his.

2. He immediately obeyed the call to "follow" without demanding to know all the specifics of his journey.

3. He walked by faith instead of by sight.

4. He did not allow fear of the unknown to keep him from traveling his course.

5. He continued to move according to God's Word, not his own emotions.

6. He sought the Lord's guidance and honored Him through worship.

7. He realized early on who was in charge of his course.

Sisters, may we apply the same principles to God's calling on our lives. Let us move forward with an unwavering faith, following God's leading as we walk our God-ordained paths.

Day 2: Our Egypt

While driving to college one day, I passed a house where several family members were playing in the front yard. At the precise moment that I noticed the scene, my heart was completely drawn to this appealing image. The family seemed happy and appeared to be safe. By contrast, my situation at the time was one that involved great distress. How in the world had my family arrived at such a place?

In the midst of this circumstance, fear had so engulfed my life that running appeared to be the best solution. With circumstances spiraling out of control, I decided to return to a place I felt would be safe in order to escape the current problem. However, in all truthfulness, it was an area from which God had removed me years prior with no call to return.

For a time, my new dwelling became my Egypt—the place I retreated to for safety and security instead of going to God. Yet, what I turned to for security, God regarded as wrong. I was living in complete disobedience. Misery soon followed, and a severe restlessness invaded my soul. My peace had long since evaporated. In time, and through God's grace and intervention, He would bring me back to the area He had given to both my children and me to dwell.

During our journeys, periods will occur when our very own Egypts will beckon us to return. It may appear in the form of ungodly friendships attempting to draw us back to our past or as old behaviors bidding us to compromise. When such moments arise, it is wise to allow God to answer their summons.

In the biblical narrative of Genesis 12, Abram had both arrived and settled in the land of Canaan. However, when a famine swept over the land, the man of God reacted in fear instead of responding in faith. His response to this crisis drove him to seek refuge in Egypt.

Let us pick back up today with Genesis 12:10-20.

According to verse 10, what events motivated Abram to flee to Egypt?

Can you remember a time when you allowed a crisis to drive you away from the will of God? If so, what was the result?

After arriving in Egypt, what specific matter concerned Abram?

In what ways did he attempt to manipulate the situation for his benefit? What resulted from his course of action?

According to verse 16, what gifts were bestowed on Abram? How did God intervene in the crises caused by Abram?

Who scolded Abram for his deception?

Do you remember the highlights from day one? Consider some additional insights from today's text:

1. Abram did not trust God to provide for his family in the land to which God had moved him.

2. He ran to Egypt where he sought security.

3. After fleeing, he was met by yet another obstacle.

However, instead of trusting the Lord to take care of him, he lied to protect himself, putting his wife in danger.

At this point in Abram's journey, his response was quite different. For a time, not only did his journey take him in a different direction, but so did his faith. At the beginning of Abram's journey, God was in control. However, as time passed, Abram had taken more control as he attempted to plot his own course.

Often, when a crisis comes, it can affect many aspects of our journeys if handled in an unbiblical manner. I remember being called to a particular place to serve. At first it was wonderful, and I enjoyed my work. Yet, over a period of time, I became the target of another person's attacks. One day, as the individual confronted me once again, I said to God, *It's never going to change,* and I ran. However, weeks after I made the decision, God began to convict my heart. He showed me clearly that I had left the situation prematurely instead of allowing Him to intervene. My journey had been altered because of my lack of trust in God and because I had trusted in my own understanding of what needed to happen. I ran to my very own personalized Egypt.

Our Egypt

Places that appear safe and appealing. In his article, "Hagar the Egyptian: A Note on the Allure of Egypt in the Abraham Cycle," Iain Duguid states, "The Egyptian option, while apparently attractive, always leads to disaster in the long run."[1]

During our journeys, we will always encounter difficult periods. How we respond in such moments is crucial. Leaving a God-assigned place to find temporary relief in our Egypt can produce devastating consequences. Even though the Lord showed grace to Abram and his family while they stayed in Egypt, Abram would leave that place, bearing consequences that would last a lifetime.

Look back at Genesis 12:16. While residing in Egypt, Abram gained both "male and female" servants. In light of Genesis 16:1, this may have been the time when Abram acquired a young woman named Hagar. If so, we will see in Week 2 additional consequences of Abram's journey to Egypt.

> **Are you currently residing in Egypt? If so, briefly explain how you came to such a place.**

We never have to run from our circumstances. If you have currently found yourself in Egypt, you do not have to stay there. God in His love and grace will move you to the place He has for you to dwell if you allow Him to take the lead.

---

1   Iain Duguid, "Hagar the Egyptian: A Note on the Allure of Egypt in the Abraham Cycle," *Westminster Theological Journal* 56, no. 2 (Fall 1994): 420. Used with permission.

Day 3: Returning to Our First Love

While lying on my bed one evening, I began to read the Word of God. I found myself drawn to the story of Boaz and Ruth. As I read the book of Ruth, I was overcome by a strong sense of God's love for me. I had never felt so safe and so cherished.

At this particular time, I was mired in a pit of sin. Yet, instead of returning to my Father, I continued down the same sinful path until God's redeeming love collided with my rebellion, and my sinful lifestyle came to a halt.

In brokenness and repentance, I knelt before the Lord in the middle of my den. Instead of running from Him, I ran back to Him. I returned to my first love, to a place I had longed to reside.

As we discussed on day two, Abram left the Promised Land during a famine in order to travel to Egypt. Yet, the Lord would not allow him to remain there. Let us pick up today's reading in Genesis 13:1-4.

> **So Abram went up from Egypt to the Negev, he and his wife and all that belonged to him, and Lot with him. Now Abram was very rich in livestock, in silver and in gold. He went on his journeys from the Negev as far as Bethel, to the place where his tent had been at the beginning, between Bethel and Ai, to the place of the altar which he had made there formerly; and there Abram called on the name of the LORD.**

Go back to verse 1 and underline, "went up from Egypt."

Now, look once more at verse 3 to the underlined words: "He went on his journeys from the Negev as far as Bethel to the place where his tent had been at the beginning, between Bethel and Ai." Abram was on his way back to God's appointed place for him, the place where He had previously settled, worshipped, and called upon God.

The Beginning

Do you remember those sweet times with the Lord when you first accepted Him as Savior? Do you recall seasons where you got off-track, yet repented, only to be brought once again into a right relationship with Him? Abram had not only returned to his rightful place; he had also returned to the will of God.

> **According to verse 4, what important action did he take after arriving back in the land of Canaan?**

Returning to Our First Love

I want us to look at Revelation 2:1-7. Take time and ponder God's message in this passage.

Jim Wicker stated,

> *These letters to the seven churches (chs. 2-3) are from Jesus and recorded by John. Each one begins with a beautiful description of Jesus from Rev. 1:13-20. The first letter is to*

the Ephesus Church, and it describes Jesus as holding "the seven stars" in His "right hand" and walking among "seven golden lampstands" (2:1). What does this mean? Revelation is full of meaningful symbols, and most of them are described in the verses around them (their context). In 1:20 we read that the stars are the "angels of the seven churches" and "the lampstands are the seven churches." The Greek word for angel [angelos] can also mean "messenger." Since each of the seven letters are written to the "angel" of each church—that most likely means the pastor. Jesus walks among the churches and holds the pastors in His right hand (the place of power). He is at work among us, cares for us, and has plans for us![2]

Review verses 2 and 3. Take a few moments and underline the encouraging attributes the Lord affirms in His people's behavior (the Church).

In the midst of all the good the Lord notices within His Church, what is the number one concern He expresses in verse 4?

Wicker continued,

> *Jesus mentioned some great deeds of the Ephesian church—they had an exemplary past (vv. 2-3). For someone visiting their church, they likely looked outwardly impressive. They appeared to be a noteworthy church in a very important city. But Jesus knew they had inward problems. They were going through the motions but doing so with wrong attitudes and an improper focus. Verse four says they had left their first love (Jesus). Imagine that! They seemed to be serving Jesus, but they forgot about Him. That is like giving a birthday party but neglecting to invite the honoree.*[3]

When a single mother finds herself drifting as a result of rebellion or stagnant due to the busyness of life, God will always point to the heart of the matter.

First Samuel 16 records a story about a prophet named Samuel. God sent him on a mission to anoint the next king of Israel. Yet even though Samuel had no idea who the appointed man would be, he followed God's call and moved forward in obedience to His instructions.

> **And the LORD said, "Take a heifer with you and say, 'I have come to sacrifice to the LORD.' You shall invite Jesse to the sacrifice, and I will show you what you shall do; and you shall anoint for Me the one whom I designate to you." (1 Samuel 16:2-3)**

Go back and underline, "you shall anoint for Me the one whom I designate to you."

Samuel arrived at the location where the Lord directed him, and the search for the next king of Israel began. As Jessie's sons entered the room, Samuel's eyes settled on Eliab. Immediately he concluded that the young man was the Lord's chosen vessel because of his outward appearance. However, he could not have been more wrong. Notice the Lord's response to the prophet's assumption: "But the LORD said to Samuel, 'Do not look at his appearance or at the height of his stature, because I have rejected him; for God *sees* not as man sees, for man looks at the outward appearance, but the Lord looks at the heart'" (1 Samuel 16:7).

---

2   Jim Wicker, professor at SWBTS, personal communication, 2018, at the writer's request. Used with permission.
3   Wicker, personal communication.

> **Go back and highlight, "for God sees not as man sees." According to God, at what does man look?**

> **Go back and underline, "but the LORD looks at the heart." How does this passage of scripture speak to you personally?**

Revelation 2 describes the Church of Ephesus as a body that engaged in a lot of great deeds. Yet something was missing, and Jesus knew what it was. He drew their attention to the true condition of their hearts.

I remember the day a friend reached out asking for prayer. "My heart is numb," she stated. "I don't know what is wrong." As I prayed with her and for her, Revelation 2:4 came to mind. My sister in Christ had left her first love. Yet, little did she realize that *He had never once left her.* He was awaiting her return.

According to Revelation 2:5, what three tasks did Jesus give to the Ephesian Church? (1) To "remember" from where they had fallen, (2) to "repent," and (3) to "do the deeds" that they "did at first."

Wicker explains, "Proverbs 28:13 covers the first two actions and can be summarized as 'admit it and quit it.' You are to remember your sin and own up to it. Next, you must turn away from that sin and turn to Christ. This is what it means to repent. Finally, you are to serve Christ like you used to before you left your first love."[4]

> **How can you apply verse 5 to your life?**

Valentine's Day has always been a little hard for me. I imagine it is for many people. However, on one particular holiday, it became quite special. On this precise Valentine's Day, I headed out early for a quick workout and to run a few errands. It was a beautiful sunny day, so I took my time, went out to eat, and then walked leisurely through a stunning college campus. As I prepared for the stroll, a particular song came to my mind: "Take Me to the King." Over the next forty-five minutes, the Holy Spirit poured into my soul as I listened repeatedly to the lyrics.

After returning from these daily activities, I pulled into my driveway on the seminary campus. As I started texting many single moms to wish them a Happy Valentine's Day, my attention was caught by a scene that perfectly illustrated the holiday, one which I watched from a distance.

A young woman walked over to greet what appeared to be either her boyfriend or her husband as he waited on the curb, holding a single red rose. He looked up at her with a face reflecting so much love for his lady. As she reached out to take his special gift, no words were needed on her behalf. Her face conveyed it all. I smiled to myself while turning away to give them privacy in their special moment.

---

4   Wicker, personal communication.

As I sat in my car, I was granted a moment of my own. I began to ponder the love of God as I sensed His very near presence. In that instant, there was no rose, no balloon, and no box of candy. Instead, in its place was something much greater. A peace overtook any worries or concerns that attempted to disquiet my heart. A deep-rooted joy was present that only God Himself could bestow, and there was a heart spilling over with love from my One and only Valentine, Jesus. This One who gave His life on a cross so that a world could know Him as Savior, met me in a way I would never forget. No number of roses could have matched what I was given on this day from the One who created love, from the One who is love.

Where do you find yourself today? Are you at the feet of Jesus or overwhelmed with numerous tasks? Are you living victoriously for Him, or are you knee-deep in unrepentant sin? Are you preoccupied with a ministry task or seeking to know Him more? Today, if you have left your first love, your Father is awaiting your return. He is only a prayer away (Revelation 2:5).

Day 4: An Eternal Perspective on Conflicts

Throughout our journey, conflicts are certain to arise. Feelings will be hurt, friendships will come and go, and people whom we deemed "trustworthy" may betray us. Yet, the way we respond to such conflicts will either reflect a loving Savior or a deceitful enemy. Our reactions to others can leave wonderful impacts or devastating consequences.

I remember one particular period when a certain individual caused some hardship in my life. Instead of confronting the person in grace and in love, I ignored the attack and moved on. However, I did more than just overlook a hurt. I completely disregarded the person who had caused the pain.

I had no idea at the time that my behavior toward the lady was being observed by a young Christian woman. One day while she and I were visiting, she made a comment about how I had dealt with people who had hurt me. Her description of my behavior revealed an area that did not reflect Jesus or His love to others. To my surprise, the young lady had been impacted negatively by my behavior.

By contrast, a pastor's wife walked into a sanctuary one evening to attend a church function. As she was fellowshipping with other believers, she responded graciously to someone's negative comment. The disgruntled speaker was quickly offended and lashed out. The pastor's wife responded with grace and in gentleness. In front of others, she quickly apologized to the woman she had offended. When I heard the story, I was greatly impacted by the woman's response. She humbled herself before others and allowed her Father to control her reaction, thereby bringing glory to His name instead of calling attention to herself.

People constantly observe our behavior. They watch how we respond to hurtful comments. They notice whether we withdraw or express grace to those who have wounded us. Therefore, we must understand the importance of holding to an eternal perspective in conflicts in order to first and foremost glorify our Savior, as well as to reflect Him to those who are watching.

Let us pick back up today with the story of Abram. On day three, we studied his return from Egypt to the land of Canaan. Today, we will look at yet another trial he encountered. Read Genesis 13:5-13.

According to verses 5–6, what problem had developed between the herdsmen?

Use verse 7 to describe the conflict.

At this point in the passage, we see only the surface of the problem. God had blessed both Abram and Lot with great possessions. However, the particular section of land they dwelt in could no longer hold both families and their belongings. Therefore, a solution to the problem was necessary: one which resulted in God being glorified, one which required a dying to self and personal rights, and one which reflected a genuine love for a brother in the Lord.

Who took the initiative to rectify the situation? Abram or Lot?

Notice Abram's humble plea to Lot in response to the crises: "Please let there be no strife between you and me, nor between my herdsmen and your herdsmen" (Genesis 13:8). How many friendships, relationships, and family ties could be mended today if we approached differences the way Abram did? Never once did he demand his own way or attempt to blame anyone for the contention. Instead, he put the needs of others before his own in order to make peace (Romans 12:18). Though friction had occurred, Abram reminded his nephew of a very important truth: "We are brothers."

How many times do we go through life cultivating bitterness instead of taking measures to mend wounds? How often do we look at those in the Christian faith as enemies instead of as brothers and sisters in Christ? Abram had an eternal view as he dealt with this dispute. My friends, we must do the same when we face conflicts.

In order to settle the strife, what suggestion did Abram offer Lot?

Did you notice how Abram put his nephew's well-being before his own? Take a look at Philippians 2:3-4: "Do nothing from selfishness or empty conceit, but with humility of mind regard one another as more important than yourselves; do not *merely* look out for your own personal interests, but also for the interests of others."

What is the Philippians text instructing us to do?

> **In what areas can you apply these truths to your life?**

Following Abram's stance, a separation took place between him and Lot (Genesis 13:11). However, Lot was still a part of Abram's family, and they remained in good fellowship. Abram settled in Canaan, while Lot chose Sodom. Yet, Abram never once stopped loving his nephew. In fact, after Lot established himself in Sodom, a war broke out, and he was taken captive (Genesis 14). When this happened, Abram came to his rescue, rallying troops to bring his nephew home. There is never a greater time when a Christian reflects Christ than when he loves another person who, for various reasons, may be hard to love.

Do you have relationships in your life that involve conflict? If so, how can today's lesson help you look at this discord through a different lens? Going forward, how might you respond differently to those who cause disputes? Invite God to step on the scene of your struggles. You may be surprised at the outcome once He intervenes.

I want to conclude today's lesson with the following encouragements and biblical admonition. In the book, *Resolving Conflict Christ's Way*, Robert D. Jones states,

> *What does Romans 12:18 teach about resolving conflicts? First, you are responsible to live at peace with others. The command is clear; the responsibility is yours. Jesus imposes the same duty in His teaching, and He commands you to take the initiative in reconciling relationships. Whether you are the offending party (Matt. 5:23-26) or the offended party (Matt. 18:15-17; Luke 17:3-4), Christ calls you to go to the other person, to interface with him. The fact that these texts also call the other person to go to you must not excuse your delay ("he started it, let him come to me"). You are not responsible for his actions; you are responsible for yours—"as far as it depends on you." Let nothing derail your pursuit of peace.[5]*

REMEMBER: In obtaining an eternal view on conflicts, I leave you with the following counsel:

1. Invite God to step on the scene of your conflict, while applying Proverbs 3:5-6 to your life.

2. Seek the mind of God in regard to the conflict, and ask Him to help you view the dispute through His lens.

3. Pray for wisdom and direction on how to best approach the discord (James 1:5).

4. Spend time searching the scriptures to learn of God's truths in regard to conducting offenses biblically.

5. Wait on the Lord's instructions before moving forward to handle the situation (Psalm 27:13-14; Isaiah 64:4).

6. Above all else, seek the glory of God in and through the entire matter (1 Corinthians 10:31; Colossians 3:17).

---

5   Robert D. Jones, "Resolving Conflict Christ's Way," *Journal of Biblical Counseling* 19, no. 1 (Fall 2000): 13. For further study, see his book, *Pursuing Peace: A Christian Guide to Handling Our Conflicts* (Crossway, 2012). Used with permission.

Day 5: Walking on Our Inheritance

This week we discussed the many aspects of Abram's journey. We were inspired by his obedience to God and enamored with a faith that led him to follow God's summons to an unknown future. We were stirred by the moments of crises yet alerted to valuable lessons, which aid us in our own personal journeys. We were elated by his return to the inherited land, while encouraged by God's grace in the midst of wrong turns. Furthermore, we were impacted by his behavior in conflict as he put another person's needs above his own. All of these life-changing applications can inform our journey.

Quick Recap of This Week's Lessons

Your Calling

God has a special calling on your life. Though His design may include various experiences you never envisioned, you can always trust in His sovereign plan. As He directs your course, be obedient to His directions, even though you may not understand His guiding hand. God will always grant you His best, though at times His best may come with periods of suffering.

As God's calling on your life unfolds, trust in His timing to bring everything together for His glory and for your good. In addition, remember it is the Lord's great pleasure to use you for His kingdom work.

> **"You did not choose Me but I chose you, and appointed you that you would go and bear fruit, and that *your fruit would remain, so that whatever you ask of the Father in My name He may give to you."* (John 15:16)**

Egypt

Crises are sure to come to those who follow Christ. The way in which we deal with such periods can affect our journeys either for good or for bad. Remember, when the going gets tough—and it surely will—determine now to run to God instead of to your Egypt.

> **There is a way which seems *right to a man,* But its end is the way of death. (Proverbs 14:12)**

Returning to Your First Love

As you journey onward, you may find yourself busy with day-to-day activities that fill your time as you drift away from spending time with your Father. Or you may observe that you have been delighting more in your calling than in your relationship with Jesus or even running from your appointed path to one that looks more appealing. Nonetheless, no matter where you find yourself in this journey, Jesus longs to have you back with Him, on the path He has appointed for you to travel. Instead of running from Him, run to your first love who will never turn you away.

> **But in their distress they turned to the LORD God of Israel, and they sought Him, and He let them find Him. (2 Chronicles 15:4)**

Conflicts

As you live life, you will face periods of conflict with family members, friends, and even acquaintances. Yet, no matter where conflicts arise, it is imperative that we handle each encounter from a biblical perspective.

> **The Lord's bond-servant must not be quarrelsome, but be kind to all, able to teach, patient when wronged, with gentleness correcting those who are in opposition, if perhaps God may grant them repentance leading to the knowledge of the truth. (2 Timothy 2:24-25)**

When it comes to conflict, here are two great reminders. First, we must understand the love of God. In the book, *The Peace Maker*, author Ken Sande states the following: "The more you understand God's love and power, the easier it is to trust him. And the more you trust him, the easier it is to do his will. This is especially true when you are involved in conflict. If you believe that God is watching over you with perfect love and unlimited power, you will be able to serve him faithfully as a peacemaker, even in the most difficult circumstances."[6]

The second reminder is, when dealing with conflicts, to live under the cross in our actions and in our view of others is a must. For when we do, we will reflect the Lord Jesus, bringing glory to His name.

In closing, I want us to glean from another aspect of Abram's journey. Read Genesis 13:14-18:

> **The LORD said to Abram, after Lot had separated from him, "Now lift up your eyes and look from the place where you are, northward and southward and eastward and westward; for all the land which you see, I will give it to you and to your descendants forever. I will make your descendants as the dust of the earth, so that if anyone can number the dust of the earth, then your descendants can also be numbered. Arise, walk about the land through its length and breadth; for I will give it to you." Then Abram moved his tent and came and dwelt by the oaks of Mamre, which are in Hebron, and there he built an altar to the LORD.**

Reread verse 14, paying close attention to the underlined words. "The Lord said to Abram, <u>after</u> Lot had <u>separated</u> from him." The Lord had Abram's full attention. His focus was no longer on disagreements but instead on his heavenly Father. His ears were open, and his heart ready to receive all that God had to say in regard to his life.

Notice the instructions spoken to Abram at the beginning of verse 14: "Now lift up your eyes and look from the place where you are." Abram was being called to envision an inheritance that extended way beyond what he inhabited; one he could have never imagined in his own mind. This inheritance and its associated promises would bless not only Abram but also his descendants for generations to come.

> **According to verses 15–16, what promises did God make to Abram?**

Oftentimes, God will reveal a specific promise in His Word or remind us of the ones He has previously given. We may be in the midst of a difficult situation or engaging in daily routines, as Abram was. The

---

6   Ken Sande, *The Peace Maker: A Biblical Guide to Resolving Personal Conflict* (Grand Rapids: Baker Books, 2004), 59. Used with permission.

question is, will we believe God, even though the circumstances surrounding us appear to contradict His assurances? Abram never lived to see all that God had promised. Yet that did not stop him from believing. God brought to fruition every promise He had made to Abram. Abram's job was to walk according to God's commands rather than by sight.

Review verse 17: "Arise, walk about the land through its length and breadth; for I will give it to you." God was calling Abram to "arise" and "walk" on his inheritance.

How did Abram respond to God's invitation?

In closing, I want to draw your attention to the word *arise* in verse 14. The command required Abram to move forward as an inheritor to the promises of God. The same message God gave to Abram applies to us today. We must arise and walk on our inheritance, the foundational truths of God's promises. This obedient act will always be a part of our journey's responsibility, adjacent with blessings we will not want to miss.

Remember, our journeys are wrapped with God's unique callings. He calls us into being; He calls us to salvation; He calls us to join Him in His work of kingdom building; He calls us to follow Him, to trust Him, and to move forward with Him by faith and not by sight.

To be called by God is never to be taken lightly but instead embraced with an unwavering trust in a loving Father who has only our best in mind. Our journeys will not always be easy, but it is with certainty they will always be in God's hands. Remember, behind each call unfolds a wonderful plan, leading to your amazing destiny. Onward, sister. Much awaits you.

Notes

_____

_____

_____

_____

_____

_____

_____

_____

_____

_____

Week 2

The Call to Stay the Course

~*Check with your instructor about when to view this week's video.*

During Week 2, we will address the following subject matters, focusing on biblical truths which give direction to our lives:

Day 1: "Taking Matters into Our Own Hands" teaches truths to single moms about the dangers of manipulating circumstantial results in one's own life, or in that of a family crisis, for one's own personal gain.

Day 2: "Taking Responsibility" instructs the ladies in biblical truths that relate to the importance of taking responsibility for one's choices.

Day 3: "When Circumstances Urge Us to Quit" guides single moms toward biblical truths in helping them view difficult circumstances through the lens of Christ, instead of through the lens of hopelessness.

Day 4: "Where Have You Come From—And Where Are You Going?" will teach ladies the importance of embracing their futures with hope and confidence in the midst of harsh conditions.

Day 5: "Get Up!" instructs single moms about biblical truths relating to God's provision for both themselves and their children. Through the continued study of Hagar, ladies will observe God's faithfulness, even in the midst of others' unfaithfulness.

Day 1: Taking Matters into Our Own Hands

God had revealed His calling on my life, and with much excitement, I began to plan how this call would be lived out. I embarked upon a mission I felt the Lord had ordained. I placed my hands on various doors, striving to open each one, yet they would not budge. I continued this regimen until my energy was consumed by repeated failures. I became confused about why God was not allowing things to transpire according to His call. Yet as time passed, God in His mercy revealed the problem. I had jumped ahead of His sovereign plan. His calling was certain—His timing, however, was different than I had anticipated.

The Old Testament records the story of a young woman named Sarai, who found herself on a similar path—though in distinctly different circumstances. A promise had been made of a child to come, along with a future filled with blessings. However, an anxious heart would entice Sarai to attempt to usher in what God had promised long before His appointed time.

Abram had arrived in the land of Canaan and was blessed by God. Reflect once more on Genesis 12:2: "And I will make you a great nation, And I will bless you, And make your name great; And so you shall be a blessing."

God had promised to make a nation out of Abram and his descendants. Yet, there seemed to be a slight glitch in the unfolding of this promise, so Abram brought this problem before the Lord. Read Genesis 15:1-6.

> **According to verse 1, what did God tell Abram?**
>
> **According to Genesis 15:2-3, what question did Abram ask God? And what did he assume?**
>
> **What was God's answer to Abram in Genesis 15:4?**
>
> **Take a few minutes and write out God's words to Abram in verse 5.**
>
> **According to verse 6, how did Abram respond to God?**

God assured Abram that He would give him the promised child. However, it would not be Eliezer. Instead of casting doubt on God's promises, Abram believed Him (Genesis 15:6). Yet, as time went by and the fulfillment of the promise was delayed, Sarai became restless and took matters into her own hands instead of waiting on God.

Read Genesis 16:1-4 and answer the following questions.

> **According to verses 1–2, what was the trying circumstance in Sarai's life, and to whom did she credit her condition?**
>
>
> **According to verse 2, what request did Sarai make of her husband?**
>
>
> **Why was Hagar summoned to be Abram's wife?**

Notice Abram's response with regard to his wife's request: "And Abram listened to the voice of Sarai."

> **What problem do you see with not only Sarai's request but Abram's response? Look back once more at your answers from Genesis 15:1-6. (1) Abram was promised descendants. (2) God made it clear that a child would come through Abram and Sarai. (3) Abram "believed God."**

As the promise continued to go unfulfilled, Sarai implemented her own plan. She crafted a proposal that would exacerbate her existing problem. Furthermore, Abram agreed to participate in the scheme.

> **How often do we attempt to fix our own problems?**

In high school, Melinda had dreamed about marrying and having a big family. She was a Christian and, for the most part, had lived her life for Christ. Yet, during a time of rebellion, she pursued a relationship not ordained by God. She fulfilled her dream, but not in the way God had planned. Today, after much heartache, Melinda has learned the importance of waiting on God's best instead of attempting to manufacture His blessings in her own strength.

> **Has there ever been a time when you took matters into your own hands instead of trusting the situation to God? What was the outcome?**

Read Isaiah 64:4:

> **For from days of old they have not heard or perceived by ear, Nor has the eye seen a God besides You, Who acts on behalf of the one who waits for Him.**

Re-read Isaiah 64:4 and fill in the following blanks:

> For from days of _____ they have not _____ or _____ by ear, Nor has the _____ seen a God besides _____, Who _____ on behalf of the ___ who _____ for Him.

> **How does this verse offer hope to those who are waiting on God to act on their behalf?**

> Trust in the LORD with all your heart And do not lean on your own understanding. In all your ways acknowledge Him, And He will make your paths straight. (Proverbs 3:5-6)

> **According to this passage of scripture, what is God asking us to do, and what promise does He give if we carry out His directives?**

Instead of waiting for the fulfillment of God's promise, Sarai decided to manage the situation herself in hopes of gaining a guaranteed outcome. Yet, as we study the remainder of this story, we will see the devastating consequences of Sarai's choice to move ahead of God's timing.

At times, our journeys will include periods of waiting for God's interventions, His answers, His directions, and His fulfillment of promises. Yet during such seasons, if we are not careful, we might find ourselves trying to manipulate the situation in order to bring about our desired outcome. We may be tempted to step in and take over. However, we should diligently guard against such temptations.

Let God intervene in your situation today. Take the matter you are facing out of your hands and entrust it to the Lord's care. You will certainly be glad you did.

Day 2: Taking Responsibility

Difficulties arise during assorted periods in our lives. These seasons will come for various reasons and from a variety of sources. Some will be straightforward and painless, while others will be more complicated. However, in the midst of such trying circumstances, one unshakable truth remains—God will cause all things to work together for good for those who love Him and are called according to His purpose (Romans 8:28).

Tribulations originate from diverse sources. Some come directly from the hands of God. At such times, God allows suffering in a person's life for a greater purpose than he or she may perceive at the time. We see this in the life of Job when God gave permission for Satan to launch a full-blown attack on a faithful man. The result of such a trial? Job's life was transformed.

During particular periods, individuals undergo pain as a result of the sins of another person against them. I know of several young men who agonize to this day over the absence of a dad who continues his drug addition, robbing his sons of a loving father. Likewise, some face betrayal from individuals they love, while others encounter emotional and physical abuse through no fault of their own.

Last, some persons suffer because of their own poor choices. David was a man after God's own heart. Yet, in a moment's time, he gave way to temptation and experienced devastating consequences (2 Samuel 11-12).

Unfortunately, I am one of those persons who made a number of poor choices. The decisions I made yielded painful after-effects for years. Yet instead of taking ownership of my sin, I spent a long period blaming others for my course of action.

Abram's wife, Sarai, not only took matters into her own hands, but she blamed the outcome of her choice on her husband. I want us to take a few moments to review once more, as we did on day one, Genesis 16.

Read Genesis 16:1-6.

Look once more at verse 2, paying close attention to Sarai's request.

> **So Sarai said to Abram, "Now behold, the LORD has prevented me from bearing children. Please go in to my maid; perhaps I will obtain children through her." And Abram listened to the voice of Sarai.**

Notice Sarai's desperation as she appealed to her husband. "Please go," she implored. Once again, whose idea was it for Hagar to be brought in to Abram? It was Sarai's.

According to verse 4, what happened as a result of Sarai's plan? How did Hagar respond to Sarai after giving birth?

According to God's Word, when Hagar had conceived the child, she despised Sarai. In other words, Hagar looked down on Abram's wife because she could not have a child, and this did not sit well with Sarai.

According to verses 5–6, who did Sarai blame for Hagar's mistreatment, and how did Abram respond to his wife's anger?

John MacArthur stated, "Sarai, not anticipating contemptuous disregard by Hagar (v. 4) as the result of her solution for barrenness, blamed Abram for her trouble and demanded judgment to rectify the broken mistress-servant relationship. Abram transferred his responsibility to Sarai, giving her freedom to react as she wished (v. 6)."[7]

The following story is shared in hopes of introducing important truths, which have brought such freedom to my life. I remember as if it were yesterday, complaining on the phone to a pastor about a situation I was facing. I had committed a transgression against the Lord and was now enduring the consequences of the act. I had repented of my sin and was walking in the forgiveness of Christ. However, I was still suffering as a result of my poor choices.

As the pastor listened attentively to my moans, he finally stated in love, "Shea, there will always be consequences to our sin." As the minister continued to communicate truth, God taught me several valuable lessons I will never forget.

---

7   John MacArthur, *Unleashing God's Truth, One Verse at a Time*, MacArthur Bible Commentary. (Nashville: Thomas Nelson, 2005), 36. Used with permission.

First of all, our transgressions reap consequences. Second, we must be willing to walk through them with a God-honoring attitude. Third, even in the midst of the repercussions, God will never refrain from being less of a loving Father, even if we have caused the catastrophe we are facing. Fourth, the Lord will walk alongside us as we live out the consequences of our poor choices. Last, as stated previously, God promises in His Word that He will work all things together for our good (Romans 8:28). To this day, I hold these insights in my heart. For even now, I still face repercussions from my wrong choices.

When we are going through difficult times, we must bear up under what God has ordained or allowed, leaning on Him for strength and endurance. When we face suffering due to another person's actions, we must obey God in how we handle such trying periods. We may not have caused the hurt, but we are accountable for how we respond to it.

In addition, if you are in an abusive situation, please seek help for both you and your children through appropriate means. Whether it be a shelter for your family or contacting law enforcement for protection, you must take action to keep everyone safe.

Finally, let me conclude with a few more insights. When we are suffering because of personal sin, we need to take responsibility for what we have done. We must repent of our sin, while knowing for certain forgiveness will be granted by a loving Savior. "If we confess our sins, He is faithful and righteous to forgive us our sins and to cleanse us from all unrighteousness" (1 John 1:9). Furthermore, our duty is to make restitution for any wrongs we have committed.

Sarai was an angry woman. Instead of admitting that her plan was wrong, she justified her sin by blaming others. Yet, what might have happened had she just admitted her wrong and repented? The heart of the matter was the matter of the heart. Sarai's heart was not right with God. Jesus stated, "For his mouth speaks from that which fills his heart" (Luke 6:45).

I remember sitting beside a single mom and listening to her bare her soul as she talked about her past. Both she and her boyfriend had stepped over some lines, dishonoring God as well as themselves. As time passed, the young woman discovered she was pregnant. Yet, to her surprise, the father revealed he was not in love with her and did not want to get married. He would, however, bear his responsibility for the care of the child, and he did.

Over time, the mom allowed anger to take over her heart. She attempted to keep the child away from the father and was very uncooperative. She punished the father for not loving her, even though he loved his child and took care of him faithfully through child support and through investing in his life as a dad. Yet, still, the mother continued to blame everything she had faced on everyone else without looking within herself.

Ladies, please do not miss the message in this story. I am not saying the father handled everything correctly. He did not. Yet, neither did the mom. In talking with the dad, he admitted he had behaved poorly and regretted it so much. She, on the other hand, never uttered a word about her own part in the situation.

When we play the blame game, we miss out on many opportunities for growth. When we spend time looking at other's faults instead of our own, we quickly find ourselves with self-pitying, vengeful, and angry hearts.

> **Why do you look at the speck that is in your brother's eye, but do not notice the log that is in your own eye? Or how can you say to your brother, "Let me take the speck out of your eye," and behold, the log is in your own eye? You hypocrite, first take the log out of your own eye, and then you will see clearly to take the speck out of your brother's eye. (Matthew 7:3-5)**

Ladies, let us cease from participating in the blame game. And may we refrain from transferring the responsibility of our actions upon another's shoulders. May we instead bring it all to Jesus.

Day 3: When Circumstances Urge Us to Quit

I was sitting on my bed writing one day when my cell phone went off. It was a text from a friend who was struggling deeply. She was a college student and a single mother. The circumstances gathering around her all indicated that she should stop her journey. I immediately called my friend to encourage her and to take her to God's Word. As we spoke on the phone, she began to list all the things that had happened to her over the span of a few weeks. The enemy's mission was clear, as he was attempting to use these events to stop her in her tracks. The Lord's mission was even clearer, for He wanted to use what she was going through to build her character, her perseverance, and her faith.

> **It is imperative that we learn to look at what we are facing through the lens of scripture. Can you recall a time when your life seemed to be falling apart? How did you respond, and what was the outcome?**

Let us pick back up today with the story of Hagar. Read Genesis 16:5-7:

> **And Sarai said to Abram, "May the wrong done me be upon you. I gave my maid into your arms, but when she saw that she had conceived, I was despised in her sight. May the LORD judge between you and me." But Abram said to Sarai, "Behold, your maid is in your power; do to her what is good in your sight." So Sarai treated her harshly, and she fled from her presence. Now the angel of the LORD found her by a spring of water in the wilderness, by the spring on the way to Shur.**

> **According to verse 7, where did the angel of God find Hagar?**

Hagar was fleeing from her mistress. She was on the run, afraid and uncertain about what to do next. Yet, something very important is worth noting from this scripture passage. Did God wait on Hagar to get her life together before He came to her? No. Did he scold her because she was running, hurting, or fearful? No. Instead, God met her in her brokenness.

Read the following scripture passages:

> **The LORD is near to the brokenhearted and saves those who are crushed in spirit. (Psalm 34:18)**

> **According to verse 18, to whom is God near?**

He heals the brokenhearted And binds up their wounds. (Psalm 147:3)

According to verse 3, what does God promise to do for people who are broken?

Over the next three days, we will look at Hagar's *circumstances*, her *condition*, and her *calling*.

Today, we will focus on her circumstances:

1. Hagar was used to bear a child.

2. She was not loved by Abram as Sarai was.

3. She was harshly treated by a person whom she served.

4. In the midst of her mistreatment, the Bible does not record anyone who stood by her.

5. She was now fleeing for her life with nowhere to go and no idea of what to do.

6. She was pregnant with no job, no home, no food, and no direction.

7. Last, Hagar played a part in her own suffering as a consequence for her disrespectful treatment of Sarai.

Hagar was in a tough situation, facing things that would have caused most women to give up. *Give up* is what she might have done had it not been for God's intervention. He knew where she was, what she needed, and how He was going to provide.

Satan uses circumstances in a person's life to attempt to interject fear. He plants seeds of doubt in the hearts of God's children with hopes that they will distrust their heavenly Father's love and ability to rescue them from their trials. However, God takes circumstances in His children's lives and uses them as tools to make them more like His Son, Jesus. The world's perspective on trials is much different than God's (James 1:2-4 and Romans 5:1-5). For the Lord's standpoint is one of growth for His children and glory for Himself.

Read John 9:1-3:

> **As He passed by, He saw a man blind from birth. And His disciples asked Him, "Rabbi, who sinned, this man or his parents, that he would be born blind?" Jesus answered, "It was neither that this man sinned, nor his parents; but it was so that the works of God might be displayed in him."**

According to John 9:1-3, man's view of this suffering was that someone sinned, and that sin caused this blindness. God's view was, "So that the works of Himself might be displayed in him."

Again, we must seek God's mindset when facing difficult circumstances. John MacArthur reminds us that when we think as God thinks, we are thinking like Scripture. He references this truth to Colossians 3:16.[8]

---

8   John MacArthur, *Think Biblically* (Wheaton, IL: Crossway Books, 2003), 51.

> **What circumstances are you facing?**

> **How are you choosing to view these circumstances?**

Ask the Lord to give you His mindset on what you are currently facing. Ask to see your circumstances through His eyes.

Hagar was in a desperate situation. All she could see was her overwhelming need. Yet from God's vantage point, there was no need for distress because He was near. In her desperation, God intervened, and Hagar's hopelessness was replaced with hope. She was met by a loving Father who would soon turn everything around for her good.

We are not called to look at our circumstances in order to understand our situation. Rather, we are invited to look to God and trust Him in those difficult seasons as we move forward with Him.

> **Therefore, if you have been raised up with Christ, keep seeking the things above, where Christ is seated at the right hand of God. Set your mind on the things above, not on the things that are on earth. (Colossians 3:1-2)**

Day 4: Where Have You Come from—And Where Are You Going?

Of all the hindrances that keep people from walking with Christ, bondage to their yesterdays is one of the greatest. Many individuals find themselves stuck in their pasts, while longing for their tomorrows. Instead of living the abundant life, people are merely coping with unhealed hearts and emotions that give way to captivity. However, this is not God's plan for His children. "We are more than conquerors," says the Lord. Yet, many of us are living as defeated victims.

For years, I lived in the shame and guilt of past failures instead of in the freedom Christ gives. I listened to the lies of the enemy more than to the certainties of God's Word. Over time, I came to understand two important truths. First, God's Word always trumps the enemy's message. Yet, I must choose to believe God instead of doubting Him. Second, one of Satan's greatest goals is to keep people enslaved to their past in order to keep them from experiencing God's liberty. After coming to these realizations, I knew with certainty that I no longer had to dwell in my past. Those sins were paid for on the cross of Christ, and I was to live as a cleansed vessel, useful to God.

Read Genesis 16:6-8.

Today I want us to shift our focus to the questions the angel asked Hagar in Genesis 16:8. Remember, Hagar was in the middle of a desert. She was feeling alone, afraid, and abandoned. Yet in the midst of a tough situation, God intervened. Take a few moments and reread Genesis 16:8. In this text, the angel asked, "Hagar, Sarai's maid, where have you come from and where are you going?" And she said, "I am fleeing from the presence of my mistress Sarai."

At this point in Hagar's journey, her condition was evident. She saw no way out of her circumstances. She felt hopeless and afraid.

The first question posed by the angel was this: "Where have you come from?" Was this ever a loaded question!

> **After studying her circumstances and condition, how would you answer this question if you were Hagar?**

Notice Hagar's response to the angel's first question: "I am fleeing from Sarai." She was quick to respond. Do you ever stop to think how much we focus on our trials, sufferings, and even our present circumstances? We often give more power to those things which can break our spirit than to the Spirit Himself.

> **The second question posed by the angel was, "Where are you going?" How did the fleeing woman respond to this question?**

Hagar was quick to answer the question, "Where have you come from?" but never uttered a word about where she was going. I want to be very careful about inserting my own personal opinion about her lack of response. However, I would like to make an observation, if I may. Hagar was afraid. She was without a home, and it appeared there was no place for her to go. Hopelessness had invaded her heart, and she simply sat down in her disappointment. She allowed her pain to prevent her from seeing any future.

I understand this condition, for I too have been where she was, though as a result of a different set of circumstances.

> **Have you ever found yourself in a situation where you responded like Hagar?**

At one time or another, Christians are going to face moments of despair. In the book, *The Christian Counselor's Manual*, Jay Adams reminds us that all humans—yes, even Christians—will find themselves discouraged. But it is important not to let that turn into the sin of hopelessness.[9]

People often struggle to move forward in life. They are focused on past hurts and paralyzed by the circumstances of their yesterdays. Therefore, being able to answer a question like, "Where are you going?" might appear impossible to many. Yet, because of the gospel, we can answer this question with complete confidence. Though we may be unable to see our future, we can know with certainty there is one.

If the enemy can keep us "sitting down" in our failures, or even in our desperate situations, we may never move forward to all that God has for us. "The thief comes only to steal and kill and destroy; I came that they may have life, and have it abundantly" (John 10:10).

---

9   Jay E. Adams, *Christian Counselor's Manual* (Grand Rapids: Zondervan Publishing, 1973), 40.

The enemy wants to steal your tomorrows by keeping you in your yesterdays. Jesus offers you much more, for He wants to give you "life abundantly."

In his book, *Charles F. Stanley Life Principles Bible*, Stanley talks about how we can obtain this "abundant life." It's not through wealth, power, or fame, as that will leave you feeling completely unsatisfied; rather, the only way to be completely satisfied, joyful, and thankful is through obedience to Jesus Christ and pursuing the life that He gives through salvation.[10]

While Hagar was more concerned with where she had been, God had the answer to where she was going. The Lord met a broken heart with His love, His faithfulness, and His plan. Even though she saw the future as uncertain, God definitely knew what He would do, though she could not see it at the time.

> **If you were asked the questions today, "Where have you come from and where are you going?"—how would you answer?**
>
>
>
> **Have you placed your past before a loving Father, or are you still living in light of its history?**
>
>
>
> **Do you struggle envisioning a future for you and your family?**
>
>
>
> **Have you allowed the healing touch of a Savior to heal the wounds of your heart, or are you still suffering today as a result of past sin and hurt?**

In moments of uncertainty, a person may struggle to see any hope for the future. Yet, in such desolate times, we must cling to the following truths: God has our future, our lives, and the lives of our children in the palms of His hands. Our journey is leading us toward His desired end. We can be certain He will walk alongside of us in it and through it until we all arrive home.

Day 5: Get Up

One evening, I was sitting with an older woman as she ministered the love of Christ to my brokenness. My heart was in turmoil over a situation I was facing and from which I was trying desperately to run. As her Christ-like spirit poured into my life, she began to lead me through the Word of God.

---

10 Charles Stanley, ed., *Charles F. Stanley Life Principles Bible*, NASB (Nashville: Thomas Nelson, 2009), 1545.

For close to thirty minutes, she shared her journey and all she had faced. The recent loss of a husband of many years had left her alone. Yet God was her steady hope, and nothing seemed to move this woman from her confident security in Him. During our conversation, she shared Hagar's story and God's call to return. As she did, I knew the Lord was calling me to return to a difficult situation as well.

Take a moment to remember Hagar's circumstances as well as her condition. Today, we will look forward to God's call on her life.

Read Genesis 16:8-15.

The Lord had "given heed" to Hagar's affliction. The angel not only ministered God's message to her but also conveyed specific instructions as well. She was to return and submit to Sarai's authority. Hagar was also told that she was with child, and she would bear a son. Hagar was so touched that God had noticed her and had spoken with her that she gave Him the name, "You are a God who sees." Hagar obeyed the angel's directives, and at the birth of her son, she named him Ishmael.

Let us continue to follow Hagar's journey. After the passage of several years, Hagar still lived with Sarai and Abram. Read Genesis 17, then answer the following questions.

According to Genesis 17:5 and 17:15, what significant changes had taken place in Abram and Sarai's lives?

What did God reveal to Abraham in verse 16, and how did Abraham respond to God's announcement in verse 17?

According to verses 18–19, what question did Abraham ask God, and what answer did he receive in return? What was God's original plan in this situation according to verse 21?

What did God promise to do for Ishmael in verse 20?

Read Genesis 21:1-21.

Go back and look at Genesis 21:1 and notice the underlined words: "Then the LORD took note of Sarah as He had said, and the LORD did for Sarah as He had promised."

Special Insight: No individual or circumstance can thwart God's purpose for His children. When He gives a promise, He will keep His Word. He is faithful.

Notice Genesis 21:2. The son was born to Abraham at the *appointed* time. Remember, our time is not God's time; however, God's time is always the perfect time.

How old was Abraham when Isaac was born (v. 5)?

According to verse 8, what did Abraham do when Isaac was weaned?

In verse 10, Sarah made a decision to drive Hagar and her son out from the camp. Why do you think she did so?

How did Sarah's request affect Abraham?

God had clearly told Abraham that his descendants would come through Isaac. However, Abraham loved Ishmael, and this made the separation a difficult one.

According to verse 14, what action did Abraham take?

Where did Hagar go?

This sounds like a repeat, does it not? Well, in a way, it was. Hagar found herself in a desert once again, feeling hopeless and alone. Yet this time, her son was also with her.

Reread verses 15–16. What emotions drove Hagar to take these actions?

Just as God had seen Hagar in the middle of the desert during her first flight, He saw her yet again during her second journey. As the Lord heard the lad crying, He reached out to comfort Hagar with tender love.

Write out verse 17.

In coming to them, God expressed His providential care for Hagar and her son. In addition, she was given instructions and a promise. These were a great comfort to her weary soul.

"Arise, lift up the lad, and hold him by the hand, for I will make a great nation of him." (Genesis 21:18)

As we prepare to end this week's lessons, let us conclude with key concepts that come out of this passage. First of all, the Lord told Hagar to "Arise." (He wanted her to get up. He was not finished with her. She had a future and a calling.) Second, the Lord told her to "Lift up the lad." (God had a plan for the child's life, one that included provision, and later, a family of his own.) Third, the Lord told her to "Hold him by the hand." (He wanted Hagar to take hold of her son with confidence and assurance that He would never leave nor forsake them.) Last, the Lord promised, "For I will make a great nation of him." (God had a plan for Hagar's family that extended beyond the desert.)

> **How can you apply verse 18 to your life as well as to the life of your family?**

In verse 19, God performed a miracle for the desperate woman. She was so overwhelmed by her circumstances that she could not see any way to obtain water for her and her son. Yet God opened her eyes to see something she had not previously noticed. "Then God opened her eyes and she saw a well of water; and she went and filled the skin with water and gave the lad a drink."

> **Can you recall a time when your situation and your fearful response to it blocked your vision of God's action on your behalf?**

No matter where you find yourself today, remember that just as God spoke to Hagar, He is also speaking to you in this moment. Arise; get up. Lift your child up to God. Take hold of his or her hands and move onward with God's promises and assurances for your family. This was Hagar's calling, and sisters, it is ours as well. Stay the course that God has called you to, and never give up. For on the other side of your obedience to move forward with God is more blessing than you could have ever envisioned. Don't miss what God wants to do with your life by jumping ship. Stay the course.

Notes

_____

_____

_____

_____

_____

Week 3

The Call to Courage

~Check with your instructor about when to view this week's video.

During Week 3, we will address the following subject matters, focusing on biblical truths which give direction to our lives:

Day 1: "Arise" will teach single moms biblical truths that relate to accepting the task God has laid out for their lives.

Day 2: "God Is with You" will address God's faithfulness in their journeys.

Day 3: "Be Strong and Courageous" will instruct single moms to live strong and courageously in their journeys on the basis of knowing that their strength and confidence come from the Lord.

Day 4: "Align Your Life with God's Word" will remind the ladies of the value of aligning their lives according to God's Word in every aspect of their journeys.

Day 5: "An Unlikely Candidate" will teach single moms biblical truths that relate to the Lord's unconditional love, forgiveness, mercy, and grace. Ladies will be encouraged by stories of God's redemption toward individuals who have a past, while grasping the truth that one's past never has to define one's future.

Day 1: Arise

The Lord has often spoken to my heart throughout my Christian life. In these periods, He has comforted me through various trials with messages of hope and truth as well as with promises that came along with His calling. Yet it was with certainty that these times never excluded obstacles. Of the many instances I could share, I have chosen one to give a brief highlight. It was a period that impacted me profoundly.

The Lord had been dealing with me about my participation in a particular ministry, one with numerous obstacles and uncertainties. Questions troubled my mind as I wondered how I would ever resolve the issues I faced. For a time, I endeavored to put these thoughts out of my mind and even attempted to disregard them altogether. Yet, as time went by, God began to unfold His plan. As He did, I knew I was to accept a leadership responsibility in this particular ministry. It was time to "arise" and take hold of what God was calling me to do instead of attempting to run in the opposite direction. I had almost allowed an opportunity to pass, as I was tempted to sit down in my doubts and fears instead of arising to my calling. I was called to courage in a way I would never forget.

As mentioned in Weeks 1 and 2, God had promised Abraham that his descendants would inherit the land. However, before this promise was fulfilled, a series of events would unfold, even the enslavement of his descendants in Egypt for centuries.

In their captivity, the children of Israel were subjected to hard labor for a period of over four hundred years. They cried out to God for help and deliverance. God heard their cries and summoned Moses to lead the Israelites out of slavery to the land of promise. Moses responded to God's call and led the people out of bondage.

God provided miracle after miracle throughout the Israelites' journey. From the Red Sea crossing to the manna falling from heaven, God's eye was continually on His children as He guided them toward a land flowing with milk and honey. However, in the midst of such blessings, complaints multiplied, and unbelief hardened the hearts of many (Exodus 15-18; Numbers 13-36). A journey that could be completed in two weeks turned into a forty-year period of wandering in the wilderness. During this time, many died as the result of rebellion and unbelief. However, there were two men whose obedience to God afforded them the blessing of entering the Promised Land. Those men were Caleb and Joshua.

Both men believed God when others doubted Him. God used both of them to bless His people as they moved toward the land of promise. Joshua was called to step into a leadership role, taking the place of Moses after his death. He would finish the task of leading the Israelites to their God-pledged inheritance.

Upon exiting the wilderness and entering the Promised Land, God prepared Joshua for the task, positioned him to take over, and called him to arise.

Read Joshua 1:1-4:

> **Now it came about after the death of Moses the servant of the LORD, that the LORD spoke to Joshua the son of Nun, Moses' servant, saying, "Moses My servant is dead; now therefore arise, cross this Jordan, you and all this people, to the land which I am giving to them, to the sons of Israel. Every place on which the sole of your foot treads, I have given it to you, just as I spoke to Moses. From the wilderness and this Lebanon, even as far as the great river, the river Euphrates, all**

the land of the Hittites, and as far as the Great Sea toward the setting of the sun will be your territory.

During Week 1, we discussed the calling of God. For our study this week, I want to add some additional insights with regard to God's call upon our lives.

Joshua had been called to a very important task. For years he had followed, and now, he was called to lead. Let us look briefly at Joshua's calling. Look back at verse 2:

> **"Moses My servant is dead; now therefore arise, cross this Jordan, you and all this people, to the land which I am giving to them, to the sons of Israel."**

What was the first thing God commanded Joshua to do?

What was God's second command?

God commanded Joshua to arise. The young leader probably had moments of fear that threatened to override his faith. He was following in the footsteps of Moses, and that could have been intimidating. Yet God's hand was on his life. Joshua's calling was certain, and as a result of God's summons, the future leader of Israel arose.

After losing my husband at the age of twenty-four, I too was called to arise and take on the task of being a single mom. Even though the new path filled me with trepidation, giving up was never an option. I had two little ones depending on me.

God then instructed him to cross over. God's instructions to Joshua were clear. A Promised Land was awaiting the children of Israel once they crossed the Jordan River.

Though I tackled many obstacles as a single mom, I can tell you with certainty that God brought me through each one. There were times I, too, had to cross over great obstacles in order to arrive where God was directing my children and me. He took hold of our hands, leading us every step of the way.

You and those with you. We must remember two notable truths about our calling:

1. Your calling will affect you personally.

2. Your calling will affect those around you significantly. Those who accompany you or who watch from a distance will be impacted by your steps of faith as you follow God and serve Him, no matter the cost.

To the land which I am giving to them. God continued to encourage Joshua by assuring him the land was one He had ordained for the Israelites.

Along with all the good associated with one's calling comes a word of caution.

Beware of individuals who attempt to talk you out of following God's call. Many times I found myself surrounded by people endeavoring to sway me from the very path I was being called to travel.

However, instead of allowing myself to be influenced by their discouraging words, I committed myself to the One who was calling me into His service.

The greatest responsibility we have as single mothers is first to God Himself and then to our children. The call to arise will lead us to the many paths God has called us to travel, to the numerous opportunities He has set before us, and to the amazing blessings awaiting us. Arise, woman of God. Much awaits you.

Day 2: God Is with You

Weeks after my husband's death, visitors stopped by to pay their respects and to offer well-meaning advice. I was seated in the middle of my daddy's den, listening to various kinds of counsel—how to manage money, how to raise kids, and how to handle what was in front of me. Even though I was thankful for each person's guidance, questions and fears still troubled my heart.

How would I survive being alone? Where would I move? What did I need to do for an occupation? What was my next step? As I moved forward in my journey, I continued to face uncertainties.

Months later, a lady from my church approached me to share a scripture passage she had read some days earlier. It was a verse where God promised to take special care of the widow and the fatherless. After hearing God's Word, I came to understand His protection and provision in a new way. The passage became a support I would rest on for years to come.

As we discussed yesterday, Moses had died, and Joshua had taken his place as the new leader of Israel. The Lord had commanded Joshua to arise and lead the Israelites to their Promised Land. Today, let us pick back up with Joshua 1, beginning in verse 5.

> **"No man will be able to stand before you all the days of your life. Just as I have been with Moses, I will be with you; I will not fail you or forsake you." (v. 5)**

Let us closely examine verse 5.

First Section: "No man will be able to stand before you all the days of your life."

I have had the privilege of serving in various aspects of ministry. Each opportunity has been enjoyable, with valuable lessons learned in each place of service. Yet along with the joyful periods have come times of spiritual warfare.

One day I received a phone call, and I was asked if I would meet with a group of disgruntled individuals who had questions about the ministry. I agreed. At the time of the phone call, I was out of town, so I packed my bags and headed toward the location where the meeting would take place.

As I traveled, I prayed earnestly. Before I arrived at the meeting, God spoke Joshua 1:5 to my heart. I knew I had heard from my Father, and I knew I was going to be OK. He not only protected me in the midst of their concerns but also from those who were attempting to cause me harm. God held me close during a very difficult time.

Second Section: "Just as I have been with Moses, I will be with you."

God promised Joshua that just as He had been with Moses through difficult moments and insurmountable obstacles, so He would also be with Joshua. The same holds true for us today. We are not alone as God's children. We are not alone as single moms. He is always with us.

Third Section: "I will not fail you or forsake you."

No matter how circumstances appear, God has promised He will never fail or forsake His own. As Joshua led thousands of Israelites toward their inheritance, God's promises were a secure foundation upon which the leader could stand.

> **Take a few moments to write out the third section of Joshua 1:5 in the space provided below.**
>
> **How does Joshua 1:5 speak to you?**

Take a few moments to look up the passages of scripture listed below, and then answer the following questions.

> **Psalm 37:25—What truth had the writer discovered with regard to God's faithfulness?**
>
> **Psalm 9:10—What promise is given toward those who seek God?**
>
> **Hebrews 13:5—Write out the two promises listed in this scripture.**
>
> **Matthew 28:20—What promise did Jesus make to His children?**

> **We are afflicted in every way, but not crushed; perplexed, but not despairing; persecuted, but not forsaken; struck down, but not destroyed. (2 Corinthians 4:8-9)**

Go back and underline, "but not forsaken."

The LORD is the one who goes ahead of you; He will be with you. He will not fail you or forsake you. Do not fear or be dismayed. (Deuteronomy 31:8)

> **According to this passage, who goes ahead of you? Who will be with you?**

God will never leave nor forsake His own. He never left Joshua, and my friend, He will never leave you.

> **How does claiming the promises of God for your life give you confidence in moving forward in your journey?**

Day 3: Be Strong and Courageous

I made my way down the escalators of my church toward the singles minister as fast as I could. I wanted to communicate my strong desire to speak and minister to single moms. To my surprise, he responded with a question I never expected: "Would you be willing to teach a single moms Sunday school class?" Not only was I caught off-guard, but I was simultaneously elated by his offer.

Over the next several weeks, I committed the matter to prayer. As I continued to think about the wonderful opportunity before me, my enthusiasm grew. Finally, after weeks of seeking God for direction, as well as requesting counsel from other Christians, I accepted the invitation to join God in this work.

Read Joshua 1:6.

In discussing future plans with the minister, I was given permission to name the single moms Sunday school class. While praying and seeking God for a title, He placed a particular passage of scripture upon my heart. As I continued to seek His leading, I considered the term *Strong and Courageous*. Yet, to be honest, I struggled with the name at first, while tossing others around for possible consideration. One day, I was reading the first chapter of Joshua, and as I examined verse 6, I was drawn to the significance of the word *strong*. At that moment, I knew *Strong and Courageous* was the correct name for the class of women that God would gather.

David Jeremiah explained, "Three times God told Joshua to be strong (1:6-7, 9). The word means to be 'firm, resolute, not swayed' by others from the direction to which God has called a person (1 Cor 16:13; Phi. 1:20, 27)."[11]

The Lord is not telling us to be strong in our own power, but instead, He is calling us to be resolute "in His strength," while refusing to be diverted from the path He has called us to walk.

---

11 David Jeremiah, ed., *Jeremiah Study Bible* [NKJV] (Franklin, TN: Worthy Publishing, 2013), 278. Used with permission.

God Is the One Strengthening Us

> God is our refuge and strength, A very present help in trouble. Therefore we will not fear, though the earth should change And though the mountains slip into the heart of the sea; Though its waters roar and foam, Though the mountains quake at its swelling pride. Selah. (Psalm 46:1-3)

Fill in the following blanks: God is our _____ and _____, A very present _____ in _____.

> **What does verse 2 tell us not to do?**

His Joy Is Our Strength

> Do not be grieved, for the joy of the LORD is your strength. (Nehemiah 8:10)

> **According to verse 10, what is our strength?**

God Protects His Own

> The name of the LORD is a strong tower; The righteous runs into it and is safe. (Proverbs 18:10)

> **What is promised to the righteous ones who run to the Lord?**

God Never Forsakes Those Who Seek Him

> The LORD also will be a stronghold for the oppressed, A stronghold in times of trouble; And those who know Your name will put their trust in You, For You, O LORD, have not forsaken those who seek You. (Psalm 9:9-10)

> **According to verse 10, what does God promise?**

Now open your Bibles and complete the following exercise. What does 1 Chronicles 16:11 instruct us to do?

Take a few moments and write out Isaiah 40:29.

According to Philippians 4:12-13, who did Paul recognize as the source of his strength?

How do these verses increase your confidence in God?

Look once again at Joshua 1:6, focusing on the last part:

> "Be strong and courageous, for you shall give this people possession of the land which I swore to their fathers to give them."

The Lord had promised the land as an inheritance to the children of Israel. In other words, it was a done deal. Therefore, Joshua, as well as the Israelites, had no cause to fear. God was in control of their journey as well as their inheritance. Consequently, they could be strong and courageous. Fear tends to derail us from our faith, whereas God's Word anchors us on a firm foundation of truth.

At times, as single mothers, we may become tired and even fearful. We work every day, prepare numerous meals, help with homework, and attempt to keep our homes in order. We handle problems and fret often, while feeling as though the weight of our entire family's future rests on our shoulders. Yet, we must remember valuable truths in times of weariness and fear. God is the One in control of our journeys. We are never alone, no matter how our emotions or circumstances might seem to dictate otherwise. He promises to give us strength and grace for the journey.

In closing, I want to leave with you one of my favorite scripture passages. In Isaiah 41:10, God says, "Do not fear, for I am with you; Do not anxiously look about you, for I am your God. I will strengthen you, surely I will help you, Surely I will uphold you with My righteous right hand."

Sister in Christ, stand firm in the Lord and refuse to be deterred from the path He has called you to walk. In addition, always remember, you never have to rely on your own strength. It is through Christ that we can be *Strong and Courageous.*

Day 4: Align Your Life with God's Word

I remember the day God used a pastor's wife to speak into my life about the importance of studying the Word of God. For years, I had been faithfully attending church and enjoyed reading the Bible. However, I never fully understood the significance of God's Word in bringing about growth and change. Over a span of several months, as Kathi explained the power of God's Word to change a person's life, my interest was piqued. Eventually I not only came to understand what she was talking about, but I also experienced firsthand the transforming power the Word of God can have in a person's heart.

God had given Joshua His commands while assuring him of His protection. He instructed the bold leader to be strong and courageous while reminding him of the Promised Land that awaited him. Read Joshua 1:7-9 and note the additional instructions given to Joshua.

> **Only be strong and very courageous; be careful to do according to all the law which Moses My servant commanded you; do not turn from it to the right or to the left, so that you may have success wherever you go. This book of the law shall not depart from your mouth, but you shall meditate on it day and night, so that you may be careful to do according to all that is written in it; for then you will make your way prosperous, and then you will have success. Have I not commanded you? Be strong and courageous! Do not tremble or be dismayed, for the LORD your God is with you wherever you go.**

According to verse 7, what was God's perspective on success?

How was Joshua counseled to handle the Word of God?

What was he instructed not to do in regard to God's Word?

Take a few moments to glean the truths in verse 8.

God's Word:

- It shall not depart from your mouth
- One shall meditate on it day and night
- So that you may be careful to do according to all that is written in it
- For then you will make your way prosperous
- Then you will have success

According to verse 9, God once again encouraged Joshua to be "strong and courageous." What two things did He command Joshua not to do?

What comforting truth did God communicate in verse 9?

When we align our lives according to God's Word, we are positioning ourselves to be blessed. However, when we walk according to the world's wisdom, we are setting ourselves up for failure. Joshua knew the importance of aligning his life according to God's Word.

I want to draw your attention to three of Joshua's responses as he committed himself to carrying out God's commands. First, he listened when God spoke. Second, he believed God without doubting his instructions. Last, he accepted God's timetable for carrying out those instructions.

It is one thing to hear from God, but it is an entirely different thing to act on what He says. Read James 1:23-25.

What is promised for the person who not only hears the Word of God but also does what it says? He will be blessed. Aligning one's life with God's Word entails reading, listening, believing, and obeying His teachings. Take a few moments to glean from the following truths.

Read

It is important to immerse yourself daily in God's Word (His truth brings change).

> **For whatever was written in earlier times was written for our instruction, so that through perseverance and the encouragement of the Scriptures we might have hope. (Romans 15:4)**

> **And you will know the truth, and the truth will make you free. (John 8:32)**

> **All Scripture is inspired by God and profitable for teaching, for reproof, for correction, for training in righteousness; so that the man of God may be adequate, equipped for every good work. (2 Timothy 3:16)**

Listen

As you read God's Word, pay close attention to what He is instructing you to do.

> **He who gives attention to the word will find good, And blessed is he who trusts in the LORD. (Proverbs 16:20)**

> **But He said, "On the contrary, blessed are those who hear the word of God and observe it." (Luke 11:28)**

Believe

We can always believe God's Word. He will always be faithful to His promises.

> **For this reason we also constantly thank God that when you received the word of God which you heard from us, you accepted it *not as the word of men, but* for *what it really is, the word of God, which also performs its work in you who believe.* (1 Thessalonians 2:13)**

> **And without faith it is impossible to please Him, for he who comes to God must believe that He is and that *He is a rewarder of those who seek Him.* (Hebrews 11:6)**

Obey

Applying God's Word to our lives requires us to obey what He says.

> **My son, do not forget my teaching, But let your heart keep my commandments; For length of days and years of life And peace they will add to you. (Proverbs 3:1-2)**

> **My son, give attention to my words; Incline your ear to my sayings. Do not let them depart from your sight; Keep them in the midst of your heart. (Proverbs 4:20-21)**

The Word of God is a light to His children. It is a roadmap for the journey. It is comfort and hope for weary hearts. It is encouragement for hurting souls.

Conclude this week's Bible study by reading Joshua 1:10-18.

According to verse 11, what instructions did Joshua give the people?

How many days were they to wait before they crossed the Jordan?

At the close of verse 11, what reminder did Joshua give the people?

How did the people respond to Joshua's instructions?

What encouraging words are repeated in the last part of verse 18?

Joshua took his leadership role seriously. He had followed the Lord for years, while observing His faithfulness. Now He was ready to be used for God's glory. Joshua lived His life according to God's commands and promises. Therefore, he was granted success and gained blessings throughout his journey.

Many times in my journey, all I had to lean on was the Word of God. He always proved faithful. He always came through. And my friend, He will do the same for you. Allow the Word of God to guide you, instruct you, teach you, and transform your heart. His Word will change your life. I am living proof.

Day 5: An Unlikely Candidate

I have always had a special place in my heart for the underdog—probably because I have been one. Years ago, I remember starting a vocational endeavor that was met with fierce opposition. People expressed their opinions to others about me as if to warn them that I was incapable of accomplishing the task before me. Some of the comments were reported to me, yet instead of allowing such criticisms to interfere with the project, I moved forward in spite of their lack of confidence in me. In all honesty, God used such experiences to spur me onward. I watched Him set a table before me in the presence of my enemies as He performed one miracle after another.

As we read yesterday, Joshua prepared to move the people forward. Yet before launching out, he sent two men to spy out Jericho, the first place the Israelites would conquer after entering the land of promise. In this biblical narrative, we see God's use of a person with a tainted reputation. However, we also see His call on her life—to courage, in spite of her past.

Read Joshua 2.

According to verse 1, what were Joshua's instructions to the spies?

After the spies arrived in Jericho, in whose house did they seek shelter?

How was Rahab described?

The king of Jericho had been warned that men had come to spy out the land. Where did he send his soldiers to search for the spies?

> **According to verse 4, what did Rahab do?**

Reread Joshua 2:8-11:

> **Now before they lay down, she came up to them on the roof, and said to the men, "I know that the LORD has given you the land, and that the terror of you has fallen on us, and that all the inhabitants of the land have melted away before you. For we have heard how the LORD dried up the water of the Red Sea before you when you came out of Egypt, and what you did to the two kings of the Amorites who were beyond the Jordan, to Sihon and Og, whom you utterly destroyed. When we heard it, our hearts melted and no courage remained in any man any longer because of you; for the LORD your God, He is God in heaven above and on earth beneath."**

Go back and underline all the words Rahab used to describe God's character and His activity in the lives of the children of Israel.

> **How did she describe the condition of the people in Jericho?**
>
> **What did Rahab ask of the spies on behalf of her family (vv. 12–13)?**
>
> **According to verse 14, what promise did Rahab receive?**
>
> **What did the "cord of scarlet thread" in Rahab's window signify?**

It's God's business who He chooses to use!

> **But God demonstrates His own love toward us, in that while we were yet sinners, Christ died for us. (Romans 5:8)**

"Please send me your resume," one person exclaimed. In the process of applying for jobs, I focused on my former occupations. As I thought about the places I had served, I wondered, *How can I explain my journey to anyone?*

I was overwhelmed by the consequences of my poor choices. My life's history recorded on that resume revealed more than I cared to remember. On paper I looked like a failure. Yet I had to remind myself that at the foot of the cross, I was in right standing with God.

"It is not those who are healthy who need a physician, but those who are sick; I did not come to call the righteous, but sinners." (Mark 2:17)

The more I have studied God's Word, the more I have come to realize who Jesus came to redeem. He came for sinners, those who are sin-sick and in need of a Savior. No matter what they may have been in the past, Jesus offers everyone a new beginning and a changed life that only He can provide.

In God's Word, we read about a man named Saul, who would later be renamed Paul. He was greatly feared because of his persecution of Christians. What was Saul's story? He was a schemer, a plotter of ruin, and a murderer.

Read Acts 26:9-11:

So then, I thought to myself that I had to do many things hostile to the name of Jesus of Nazareth. And this is just what I did in Jerusalem; not only did I lock up many of the saints in prisons, having received authority from the chief priests, but also when they were being put to death I cast my vote against them. And as I punished them often in all the synagogues, I tried to force them to blaspheme; and being furiously enraged at them, I kept pursuing them even to foreign cities.

Like Saul's, my own personal biography was splattered with one mistake after another. I was a person who many would have believed to be beyond God's reach. Yet God's view of me was entirely different. He took the story of Saul and used it to speak to my heart in a way I could never have imagined.

One day, Saul was on his way to Damascus, intending to persecute Christians. While on the way, Jesus Christ appeared to Saul. As a result of this divine confrontation, Saul's life was radically transformed. As he lay on the ground, blinded and afraid, Jesus spoke the following words:

"But get up and stand on your feet; for this purpose I have appeared to you, to appoint you a minister and a witness not only to the things which you have seen, but also to the things in which I will appear to you; rescuing you from the Jewish *people and from the Gentiles, to whom I am sending you,* to open their eyes so that they may turn from darkness to light and from the dominion of Satan to God, that they may receive forgiveness of sins and an inheritance among those who have been sanctified by faith in Me." (Acts 26:16-18)

What? Saul was a murderer, a troublemaker with a bad name. Yet when Jesus addressed his heart, everything changed. A new creation was birthed. I remember the day God used this passage to shine His light on a questionable situation in my life.

Remember what Jesus said to Saul and what He is saying to you and me today. Number one, "Get up and stand." Your past does not define you; God does! Number two, "For this purpose I have appeared to you." There is purpose for your life! Number three, "To appoint you a minister and a witness." God has a plan designed just for you! Number four, "Rescuing you . . . to open their eyes . . . so they may turn from darkness to light." God will use you to help others.

This passage reveals how Jesus viewed Saul and how He loved him and had a great plan and purpose for his life. The Bible records how others struggled to believe that Saul's conversion was genuine, but Jesus accepted him instantly.

What then shall we say to these things? If God is *for us,* who is *against us?* (Romans 8:31)

Take note of a very important truth. Jesus did not focus on Saul's past, and neither did Saul. It was true that he had sinned in terrible ways, but it was clear he was forgiven and called to ministry by Jesus Himself. He left his past behind and embraced His God-given future. It was a call to courage.

Some may believe others have gone too far and done too much for God to accept or even forgive them. They may say no hope exists. Yet, what you and I must remember is that God's truth speaks louder than any human words. Remember, no one is beyond God's reach—not you, not me, not anybody. This truth must take root in our hearts.

In the book, *A Theology for the Church*, Daniel Akin states, "What we can know for sure is that the God who used the innocent, shameful, despicable suffering of his own Son to reconcile the world unto himself is able to take the shards and broken fragments of our own lives and piece them together into a mosaic of beauty and wonder."[12]

In closing, I want to point you to an amazing scene recorded in the Bible. Matthew begins by recording the genealogy of Jesus. Take special notice of verse 5 where I have underlined a certain woman who is included in this line-up:

> **The record of the genealogy of Jesus the Messiah, the son of David, the son of Abraham: Abraham was the father of Isaac, Isaac the father of Jacob, and Jacob the father of Judah and his brothers. Judah was the father of Perez and Zerah by Tamar, Perez was the father of Hezron, and Hezron the father of Ram. Ram was the father of Amminadab, Amminadab the father of Nahshon, and Nahshon the father of Salmon. Salmon was the father of Boaz by <u>Rahab</u>, Boaz was the father of Obed by Ruth, and Obed the father of Jesse. Jesse was the father of David the king. David was the father of Solomon by Bathsheba who had been the wife of Uriah. (Matthew 1:1-6)**

Through the life of Rahab, as it is recorded in this genealogy, God demonstrates that our yesterdays will never alter His love or purpose for our lives. God used Rahab in a great way, as we will read later in the study, to help the children of Israel. She was a woman called to courage by God Himself. And she faithfully answered His call.

There will always be times in our lives when we too will be called to courage. Never allow fear to cause you to shrink back, woman of God. Rise up; He is calling you to courage. He is calling you to be strong and courageous!

---

12 Daniel L. Akin, *A Theology for the Church*, rev. ed. (Nashville: B&H Publishing, 2014), 201. Used with permission.

Notes

_____
_____
_____
_____
_____
_____
_____
_____
_____
_____
_____
_____
_____
_____
_____
_____
_____
_____
_____
_____
_____
_____
_____
_____

Week 4
The Call to Wait

~Check with your instructor about when to view this week's video.

During Week 4, we will address the following subject matters, focusing on biblical truths which give direction to our lives:

Day 1: "Setting Out to Move Forward" will instruct single moms through God's Word as it relates to the call to "set out" from a once-inhabited dwelling, season, or condition. In addition, individuals will be taught that setting out (from the old) will always precede a (coming-to) something new.

Day 2: "Coming to Your Jordan" will teach ladies to view their Jordans as training grounds, where some of life's greatest lessons will be taught and learned. Individuals will be encouraged to view these God-ordained seasons through the lens of hope instead of through the lens of dread.

Day 3: "Lodging at Your Jordan" will teach single moms biblical truths about waiting periods in which they will be encouraged to view these times as necessary for God's ongoing work in their lives instead of a period where nothing is happening.

Day 4: "Following God's Lead" will instruct ladies about the importance of following God and His plan versus plunging ahead and asking Him to follow their own plans.

Day 5: "Cross Over—A Miracle Unfolding" will teach single moms biblical truths that relate to God's Word being fulfilled. In addition, ladies will be directed to the following certainties: The "scene" in front of them will never derail the "plan" beyond them that God is going to bring.

Day 1: Setting Out to Move Forward

I had been offered a scholarship to attend Southwestern Baptist Theological Seminary, so I packed up my things and traveled to Texas to visit the campus in preparation for my move. For several days, I enthusiastically "viewed the land" where God was bringing me to live. I met with professors, registered for my classes, and picked out the apartment that was soon to become my new home. My heart was elated by God's gift of a Christian education as well as this chance for a new beginning. I began to anticipate the day I would actually set out from where I had been living in order to move forward to all that God had granted for my life.

The children of Israel had waited a long time to enter their Promised Land. As they camped out on the hills of Moab, Joshua realized the time was approaching to leave the place they had been camped in order to take hold of their inheritance. However, as we discussed in Week 3, before this move would take place, Joshua sent two men to spy out Jericho. For a quick recap, read Joshua 2:23-24:

> **Then the two men returned and came down from the hill country and crossed over and came to Joshua the son of Nun, and they related to him all that had happened to them. They said to Joshua, "Surely the LORD has given all the land into our hands; moreover, all the inhabitants of the land have melted away before us."**

After they heard the report, the Bible records the next actions of the children of Israel. Read Joshua 3:1: "Then Joshua rose early in the morning; and he and all the sons of Israel set out from Shittim and came to the Jordan, and they lodged there before they crossed."

This passage includes four important details:

1. Joshua rose early.

2. They "set out" from Shittim.

3. They "came to the Jordan."

4. They lodged there before they crossed.

Today, we will discuss the course of action taken by Joshua and the children of Israel.

Joshua Rose Early

The Bible states, "Joshua rose early in the morning." He knew the time had come to move forward in his journey. The dedicated leader was not only prepared to take action, but he was ready to lead the people who followed him. He did not spend time doubting if he had heard from God, nor did he question the Lord's faithfulness. He was ready to embrace his tomorrows, while leaving his yesterdays behind.

> **What inspires you most about Joshua's leadership qualities thus far?**

They "Set Out" from Shittim

Shittim—the last place where the children of Israel had arrived during their wilderness wanderings was a community where some "settling in" had taken place. This was an area where both good and bad memories had been made—a location where battles had been fought and victories won; a dwelling where many had given way to lustful desires and idol worship and in doing so became the object of God's wrath. Thus far, it had been home to over two million Israelites. Nevertheless, it was about to become "a distant land" for the children of Israel.

Years ago, I was engaged in a particular ministry of which I thought I would always be a part. It had a special place in my heart. However, over time, God began to stir my spirit. My soul was restless, and I knew God was up to something. But what?

After a year of seeking Him through prayer, He made it clear that I was to leave the current ministry I was involved in and move forward on a new course. I resigned my position, but instead of leaving the place God had called me away from, I remained. A new ministry was birthed out of my own plans. I was attempting desperately to hold on to what I wanted and what I felt was best.

As time went by, things began to fall apart. A battle of the wills took place, and through a series of events, I finally obeyed God's directions and departed. Yet, thankfully, by this time, God had accomplished His work in my heart, and I was willing to submit to His directives.

> **Has there ever been a time in your life when God called you to move from one place and transition to another? How did you respond to God's leading? Did you go willingly with a great attitude, or did you rebel against His directions? What was the outcome?**

Setting out can denote more than just leaving a particular place; it can also apply to setting aside previous patterns of living, previous friendships, or even previous hurts and regrets from the past. As described in Week 2, past choices can keep us from moving forward. Remaining entangled in the memories, comforts, regrets, or even losses of the past will always threaten the progress God desires us to make.

> **Have you ever experienced a time where you found yourself stuck in your past and unable to advance? What happened as a result?**

We should never leave past hurts unresolved. We must trust God with the regrets and memories that seek to paralyze us in their disgrace. Yet, after God's healing takes place within our lives, we must choose to move on with our Healer in spite of our feelings.

Notice Paul's admonishment to move forward. Read Philippians 3:12-14:

> **Not that I have already obtained it or have already become perfect, but I press on so that I may lay hold of that for which also I was laid hold of by Christ Jesus. Brethren, I do not regard myself as having laid hold of it yet; but one thing I do: forgetting what lies behind and reaching forward to what lies ahead, I press on toward the goal for the prize of the upward call of God in Christ Jesus.**

Go back and underline, "<u>but I press on</u>" in verse 12.

> **What was Paul's reason for "pressing on"?**
>
>
>
> **What two actions did Paul carry out according to verse 13?**
>
>
>
> **Take a few minutes to write out verse 14.**

Now take a look at Luke 9:62: "But Jesus said to him, 'No one, after putting his hand to the plow and looking back, is fit for the kingdom of God.'"

If we spend more time looking back instead of looking forward, we may miss God-given opportunities.

Ladies, our "setting out" will always be connected to our "moving forward" to the next thing God has for us. We cannot be engaged in one without the other coming in to play. God will never lead us out in order to sit us down. He has a future He is moving us toward. A providential outcome awaits us.

Day 2: Coming to Your Jordan

Many times in my life God has brought me to my own Jordan—periods filled with great difficulties and places where remaining was necessary in order for God's perfect will to be carried out. These locations served as launching pads, producing opportunities for growth and where seemingly impossible situations were miraculously resolved. God used these difficult seasons as a part of His plan to bring me to the destination He had chosen for me.

Yet even though these Jordan moments were some of the most challenging ones I can remember, they were tools in God's hand to make me more like Christ.

As we discussed yesterday, the children of Israel were on their way to the Jordan. They set out from the land of Moab to journey to their next stop. I can just picture them now as their hearts probably swung from periods of elation, as they moved closer to their inheritance, to moments of fearfulness for all the journey would entail.

The Jordan became a special place in the history of Israel. The location was where the Israelites camped before crossing the Jordan River into their Promised Land. It was a place where some of life's greatest lessons were learned. These lessons will be taught in more detail over the remainder of this week's teachings.

Read Joshua 3:1 once more:

> **Then Joshua rose early in the morning; and he and all the sons of Israel set out from Shittim and came to the Jordan, and they lodged there before they crossed.**

They Came to the Jordan

Go back and circle the words, "came to the Jordan." As we talked about on day one of Week 4, God will always "bring us out" in order to "bring us to" something new. I have listed some examples of periods where God intervened in my life by calling me out of certain situations to new and better blessings.

God Brought Me

"Out" of a sinful relationship,
"To" a renewed life.
"Out" of places I thought I would never leave,
"To" greater areas of Kingdom work.
"Out" of friendships I once believed were trustworthy,
"To" godly friends who encouraged and prayed for me.
"Out" of mentoring relationships where leaders tried to conform me to their own image,
"To" godly influences who were safe.
"Out" of situations with unsafe leadership,
"To" godly leaders who were trustworthy.
"Out" of previous hurts,
"To" forgiveness and healing.

What about you? Take a few moments to reflect on the Lord's goodness in bringing you "out" in order to bring you "to" something new.

God Brought Me

"Out"
"To"
"Out"
"To"
"Out"
"To"
"Out"
"To"
"Out"
"To"

Read Mark 5:1-20. Look closely at verse 15:

They came to Jesus and observed the man who had been demon-possessed sitting down, clothed and in his right mind, the very man who had had the "legion"; and they became frightened.

Go back and underline, "the man who had been demon-possessed" and "clothed and in his right mind." Jesus brought this man "out" of demonic possession "to" a sound mind.

The children of Israel had made it to their Jordan with a great anticipation of entering the Promised Land. However, God's next instruction would require a time of waiting before proceeding onward. They were more than willing to comply. Their past was now behind them while the future awaited them.

In closing, I want to leave you with a powerful verse that God has often used in my life to remind me of the importance of letting go of my yesterdays in order to take hold of the new thing He was doing for my tomorrows.

> **Do not call to mind the former things, Or ponder things of the past. "Behold, I will do something new; Now it will spring forth; Will you not be aware of it? I will even make a roadway in the wilderness, rivers in the desert." (Isaiah 43:18-19)**

According to verse 18, what are two things we are instructed to do?

How does verse 19 offer hope?

As we come to each Jordan in life, remember, they lie just ahead of our Promised Lands. Embrace what God is doing through those periods as He continues to move you forward toward His perfect plan.

Day 3: Lodging at Your Jordan

My friend and her husband had been serving in ministry for a number of years. However, during one particular season in their lives, they found themselves working in secular occupations. Even though they were thankful for the gift of employment, they longed for the time when God would place them back into full-time ministry. One evening the Lord spoke clearly to the couple that He would "send them" to the place He was preparing them to go. With God's spoken word came rest for the weary pair. Yet, as time went by, no doors were opening. Weeks turned into months, and before long doubt began to take root within my friend's heart. She was trapped at her Jordan, waiting.

Months later, the opportunity came for the couple to move to a different location. God was calling the pastor to a church in a neighboring county. The Lord was fulfilling the promise He had given months before. While they were waiting, they witnessed no activity on their behalf by God. Yet, He was working the entire time—not only in their hearts but in other areas as well, as He brought His plan to fruition.

Times of waiting can be some of the most difficult periods in our lives. However, God is always at work during such moments, bringing all the pieces together to implement His end goal. The question is, will we trust Him during these periods?

They Lodged There Before They Crossed

Thus far, we have discussed the Israelites "setting out" from all they had previously known and embarking upon a journey to a new location—the Jordan. Notice the last part of Joshua 3:1:

> **Then Joshua rose early in the morning; and he and all the sons of Israel set out from Shittim and came to the Jordan, and they lodged there before they crossed.**

(Go back and circle the last phrase of verse 1.) Special note: The Israelites were called to wait.

Read Joshua 3:2-3:

> **At the end of three days the officers went through the midst of the camp; and they commanded the people, saying, "When you see the ark of the covenant of the Lord your God with the Levitical priests carrying it, then you shall set out from your place and go after it." (Joshua 3:2-3)**

After the children of Israel reached the Jordan River, I wonder if the emotion of "eagerness" gripped their hearts. Perhaps they thought, *OK, we have finally arrived, let us cross*—but it was not time. Additional "actions of obedience" had to take place before they were able to proceed on their journey. Deeds are often carried out at our personal Jordans.

In the many situations I have faced in life, jumping ahead of God's timing has been the most common mistake I have made. When we know with certainty that God is leading us to carry out a particular task, we must wait for His timing before acting. When we forge ahead with our plans instead of His, we can miss the blessings and opportunities He would have brought had we waited.

Waiting periods will always be fertile ground for learning. Such intervals provide us with seasons of preparation for our callings, as well as opportunities for spiritual lessons to be learned.

Preparation for Our Calling

I had many desires with regard to ministry, and I tried to bring them all to fruition on my own. However, God had a specific plan He was unfolding for my life, one that required periods of preparation.

With regard to our calling, preparation will occur in all manner of ways and through various avenues. In my life, God called me to obtain an education, both in college as well as in seminary. However, God does not work in every person's life the same. Yet, no matter how the Lord may orchestrate your time of training, embrace such periods.

Paul was trained for his ministry as he was discipled by God Himself. Timothy gained invaluable wisdom from Paul's instructions. Priscilla and Aquila took Apollos aside in order to teach him about God. Moses lived in the wilderness for forty years as a shepherd, preparing for the day he would lead the children of Israel out of bondage.

In looking back at my younger years, I can say with certainty that I was not ready to engage in all I aspired to do. It would take years of God's working in my life to get me ready for what He was calling me to undertake.

Opportunities for Spiritual Lessons to Be Taught

During my waiting times, I learned many lessons—ones that proved essential to my growth in Christ, orchestrated by the Lord, and allowed for His glory. I would not be where I am today without such periods of instruction. To this day, I stand in awe of God's work in these seasons.

Throughout God's Word, countless mentions exist of teaching grounds. Jonah learned the importance of heeding God's call instead of running from it. Ruth was taught God's faithfulness during a period of heartache and menial labor. David witnessed God's trustworthiness as he waited to become king.

The twelve disciples were taught by the spoken words of God Himself in preparation for their callings. Waiting periods are never wasted ones.

For His Glory

God will always use times of waiting for His glory. One story illustrates this truth in a profound way. Look at John 11:1-6. Read verse 4:

> But when Jesus heard this, He said, "This sickness is not to end in death, but for the glory of God, so that the Son of God may be glorified by it."

According to verse 4, why did Jesus delay in coming to Lazarus?

Now please read John 11:17-23.

According to verse 17, how long had Lazarus been dead?

When Jesus encountered Martha, what did she say?

According to verse 23, what did Jesus promise Martha?

God's waiting times will always serve a greater purpose than what we can see with our limited views. Remember, "our ways" are not "His ways." Read Isaiah 55:8-9:

> "For My thoughts are not your thoughts, Nor are your ways My ways," declares the Lord. "For as the heavens are higher than the earth, So are My ways higher than your ways And My thoughts than your thoughts."

Joshua had led the children of Israel to the brink of the Jordan. They were only moments away from entering, so they waited and listened to God's next instructions.

Are you currently in a time of waiting? If so, how has this period affected your faith?

If you are in a waiting period, know for certain a plan is unfolding on your behalf and for God's glory. He's working. He's moving. He's intervening. Trust Him as you wait.

Day 4: Following God's Lead

In seeking a job, I had grown tired and weary while waiting. God had spoken to me with regard to my situation. Yet, instead of allowing my faith to grow while waiting, I was permitting seeds of discouragement to take root. I had sent out countless resumes only to be turned down repeatedly. However, I continued to pray for God to intervene.

As time passed, my circumstances appeared to be out of step with what I assumed God had communicated. One day, as I allowed my fear to take over, I inquired about a particular job opportunity in another state. In this time of decision, I reached out to three different advisors to seek their guidance. One stated, "As long as the door opens, walk through it." The second counseled against the move, while the third promised to pray over it. Finally, I went before the Lord.

After reaching out to God in prayer, He brought me to Joshua 3. After time with God in scripture, the Lord spoke clearly to my heart, instructing me to wait until I saw Him move. The out-of-town job search ended abruptly as I committed myself to following God's leading with regard to my future occupation.

There will be times in our journey when we will be tempted to both create and walk in our own self-made plans. However, when we choose such a path, we will bear the fruit of both confusion and regrets.

In the book, *Becoming More*, Lysa Terkeurst states, "Being driven by my plans can shift the focus of my heart from following God and being open to His unfolding invitations to following only that which leads me closer to my desires."[13] What we allow to drive us will determine the route in which we travel. We must follow God's plans, instead of asking Him to follow ours.

Yesterday we spoke of the importance of waiting on God. The children of Israel had made it to their Jordan yet for a time were called to wait before crossing. Today, I want us to look at God's next instructions to the Israelites while they lodged at their Jordan. Read Joshua 3:2-5:

> **At the end of three days the officers went through the midst of the camp; and they commanded the people, saying, "When you see the ark of the covenant of the LORD your God with the Levitical priests carrying it, then you shall set out from your place and go after it. However, there shall be between you and it a distance of about 2,000 cubits by measure. Do not come near it, that you may know the way by which you shall go, for you have not passed this way before." Then Joshua said to the people, "Consecrate yourselves, for tomorrow the LORD will do wonders among you."**

As the children of Israel were waiting, the "appointed time" to cross over drew near. Joshua sent out officers throughout the camp to relay important instructions. As noted on day three, "plunging ahead" to the Promised Land might have been tempting for the Israelites. Yet, it would have only resulted in disaster, for a wide river stood between the children of Israel and their inheritance, one that would have been difficult to cross for around two million adults and children. Yet, what appeared to be an obstacle to many became a great opportunity as God performed a miracle, one they might have missed had they moved ahead of God's time.

Look once again at verses 3–4:

> **And they commanded the people, saying, "When you see the ark of the covenant of the LORD your God with the Levitical priests carrying it, then you shall set**

---

13 Lysa Terkeurst, *Becoming More: Than a Good Bible Study Girl* (Grand Rapids: Zondervan Publishing, 2009), 208. Used with permission.

out from your place and go after it. However, there shall be between you and it a distance of about 2,000 cubits by measure. Do not come near it, that you may know the way by which you shall go, for you have not passed this way before."

Go back and underline, "When you see," "then you shall set out," "and go after it." The children of Israel were not to move until they saw the "ark of the covenant" going forward. Then, and only then, were they to set out and follow it.

The in-between times from "*when*" to "*then*" are of great significance and always connected to God's activity. Yet, so is the command, "Go after it." Many times we become fearful when the actual moment arrives. God commands us to move, yet we allow fear to immobilize us. In spite of our insecurities, when God says to "go," we must not hesitate in following His lead.

Glance back to the end of verse 4.

"Do not come near it, that you may know the way by which you shall go, for you have not passed this way before."

God cautioned the Israelites to keep a certain distance from the "ark." Why did He give such a command?

One was to respect the holiness of God, and the other was to make sure they followed the Lord's command.

In his *Life Principles Bible,* Charles Stanley discusses the Israelites' arrival at the banks of the Jordan. There were usually many routes by which they could pass through, but at this particular time it was flooded and dangerous. The Israelites were likely scared and chose to act on faith and follow the ark of the covenant, believing that's where God would lead them.[14]

God will always present us with unique and exciting opportunities. However, no matter His directional course, His plan will always prove the safest one to follow. The children of Israel were about to enter a land they had never before traveled, and it was certain they could not afford to get ahead of God. Nor can we, my friends.

In further preparation, Joshua told the priest to "take up the ark" and cross ahead of the people. He further told the children of Israel to "get ready," for God was about to do a wonder among them. He then called for the Israelites to "consecrate" themselves before crossing.

Read Joshua 3:7-10.

According to verse 7, what did God promise to do for Joshua?

According to verse 8, what instructions did God give Joshua with regard to the priests?

---

14 Stanley, *Life Principles Bible,* 303.

Joshua instructed the Israelites to "come" and "hear" the words God had spoken to him. He reminded the children of Israel that God was "alive" and "among them." In addition, He assured the Israelites of God's plan to dispossess their enemies. I can just see the children of Israel now—looking beyond where they were, as they anticipated what was to come.

Sisters, God is faithful to His own. He is moving you toward a specific destination. Do not ever doubt He has a plan. Just wait, keep praying, and watch for His activity. When He leads, follow. When He speaks, listen. And remember, He is in control of your journey, not simply assisting you in it but present with you in it.

In closing, I want to leave you with a word of caution and encouragement.

CAUTION: The Enemy's Tactics During Our Waiting and Watching Times

When we are in-between the "when" and "then" in our lives, the enemy sets up camp at our Jordan. He pulls back his bow and lets his arrows of discouragement fly.

First arrow: Look at this obstacle standing in your way. It is impossible to move.

Second arrow: Where is God? He has forsaken you.

Third arrow: Do you think He will really come through?

Fourth arrow: Are you sure you heard Him correctly? Did God really say that?

Woman of God, raise your shield of faith. No obstacle can thwart God's plan for your life, and "nothing is too difficult for Him" (Jeremiah 32:17). He has promised never to forsake you. He will come through. Stand firm on the Word of God, and take Him at His word.

WHEN—you see God move—THEN—you shall set out—AND—go after it.

Day 5: Cross Over—A Miracle Unfolding

Oh, I wish I could have seen this moment! After years of being in bondage and wandering in the wilderness in the midst of doubts, unbelief, uncertainties, and more, the time had finally come to cross over into the Promised Land. I can only imagine how elated the children of Israel were to finally reach their destination. Let us continue reading in Joshua 3:10-17.

The Israelites waited according to God's instructions. They had watched for God to move before crossing the Jordan. Finally, the time came when the priests who carried the Ark of the Covenant began to move forward, and the children of Israel followed.

Take a few minutes and write out Joshua 3:11.

Miracles

They come in all shapes and sizes. When God promises them, we are overcome by joy. Yet, as time passes and we do not see the promise carried out, we are tempted to become discouraged and even doubt what we heard. Then through God's mercy and grace, He picks us back up and causes us to hope again. And then, on a day when we least expect it, God brings about His promise.

Take a few moments and read Luke 1:5-24.

According to verse 13, what message was given to Zacharias?

According to verse 18, what question did Zacharias pose to the angel?

Look closely at verse 19 to the angel's reply to Zacharias:

> **The angel answered and said to him, "I am Gabriel, who stands in the presence of God, and I have been sent to speak to you and to bring you this good news."**

Go back and underline, "I have been sent to speak to you and to bring you this good news."

Who had sent Gabriel to speak to Zacharias?

What happened to Zacharias as a result of his unbelief?

According to verse 24, what miracle did the Lord do?

Now please read Luke 1:26-45.

According to verse 30, what message did the angel convey to Mary?

Look at verse 31 again, at the promise he made to Mary:

> **"And behold, you will conceive in your womb and bear a son, and you shall name Him Jesus."**

What concern did Mary express to the angel?

As the angel continued to speak with Mary, what important message did he convey in verse 37?

Read verse 38 again:

> **And Mary said, "Behold, the bond slave of the Lord; may it be done to me according to your word." And the angel departed from her.**

Mary believed the news that was brought to her. She based her belief on the Word of God. Look at the ending of verse 38 and fill in the blanks: "May it be done to me according to _____ _____."

God will always keep His Word. We never have to manipulate or try to make it happen on our own. God will always be faithful to His Word and to His children.

As the children of Israel crossed over the Jordan, they saw firsthand the fulfillment of God's promise to bring them to the Promised Land. For a time, it probably seemed impossible because of the circumstances surrounding them. Yet nothing was impossible for God, neither then nor today.

Look closely at Joshua 3:16. What miracle did the Lord perform?

Do you remember what Joshua told the Israelites before crossing the Jordan? They were to wait until they saw the Ark of the Covenant move forward. Remember, they were between the *when* and *then*.

What further instructions did Joshua give in verses 12–13?

A very important truth to remember: The waters did not rise up until the priest obeyed God's command. They had to step in to the water before God acted. Why? Because Joshua instructed them to do so. From where did Joshua's instructions come? The Lord. Whenever the Lord asks us to do something, we must do it. Every step of obedience will bring us closer to the Promised Land He has waiting for us. Remember, always do the next thing God tells you to do.

The miracle God promised was the miracle God delivered. In closing, read once more verse 17.

The children of Israel were called to several different waiting periods. Yet on the other side of the call to wait was the Promised Land they had so longed for. What might have happened had they disobeyed and plunged ahead of God's call to wait?

The calling to wait will not always be easy, but it will with certainty always be worth it. Wait on God, as He is preparing to lead you across your very own Jordan and into the Promised Land He has waiting for you.

Notes

_____

_____

_____

_____

_____

_____

_____

_____

_____

_____

_____

_____

_____

_____

_____

_____

_____

_____

_____

_____

_____

Week 5

The Call to Remember

~*Check with your instructor about when to view this week's video.*

During Week 5, we will address the following subject matters, focusing on biblical truths which give direction to our lives:

Day 1: "Our Gilgal" will teach single moms biblical truths when one is assigned to her own personal Gilgal. Moms will be instructed as to the significance of those times where life-changing lessons will be taught.

Day 2: "Remember" will instruct ladies about biblical certainties, which relate to the importance of remembering the Lord's work in their lives and even teach them to hold such moments as memorial stones in their minds.

Day 3: "Recall" will educate single moms about the importance of teaching their children God's truth as well as lessons the Lord has taught them throughout their journeys.

Day 4: "Rest" will remind the ladies of the importance of resting in God's promises when surrounded by enemies or even amidst difficult seasons.

Day 5: "Repositioned" will instruct single moms to view periods of being repositioned in their journeys as times ordained by the Lord.

Day 1: Our Gilgal

The children of Israel had crossed over the Jordan to Gilgal. They were now officially in the Promised Land. With their feet planted securely on their inheritance, an emotion of joy probably overwhelmed their hearts. Their journey had been a long one. Yet now they were seeing God's promises come to pass. As the Israelites awaited further instructions from the Lord, they experienced memorable moments in Gilgal, ones that were essential for their journeys as well as to their spiritual growth.

In looking back over my journey, specific periods and places stand out as some of the most influential times in my life—places where God did a tremendous work. There were instances where various chapters came to an end, while new ones offered second chances. Treasured moments were extremely impactful as God used them to conform me to the image of Christ.

Our Gilgals: Significant places which hold both precious memories and life-changing experiences; locations that are milestones in our journeys.

Join me now in studying a few examples of life-changing experiences from God's Word.

The Damascus Road Encounter: Read Acts 9:1-19.

> **Why would Paul never forget his "Damascus Road" experience?**

The Woman with the Issue of Blood: Read Luke 8:43-48.

> **What are some lessons we can take away from this story?**

The Great Catch of Fish: Read John 21:1-9.

> **What would the disciples remember most about their fishing trip?**

My Personal Gilgals

I remember helping in one particular church with a brash individual who served in a leadership role. Whenever God would use me, the person responded to me with jealousy. Instead of providing encouragement as he should have, he would make brash and unkind remarks. He would demean and embarrass people in front of others with absolutely no remorse.

Through this experience, God taught me biblically how to handle opposition. The gift of surrendering to the Lord was something I adopted and applied to my life, especially during this season. I was truly being molded into the image of Christ through suffering. Later, God moved both me and my children to a wonderful congregation with healthy leadership. To this day, this significant period holds several milestones, including "lessons learned" and "thanksgiving."

Another "Gilgal" moment consisted of a season where the Lord picked me up from a place of brokenness and set me aside for Himself. He chose this time to restore, to mature, and to fashion me into His likeness. It was a season I thought I would never survive. It was a period of significant Christian growth. To this day, I am still reaping the benefits of the change God brought to my heart during this particular season.

What about you? Can you recall a specific time/place in your life where God met you, changed you, and intervened in a way you never thought possible?

Do you still remember His work in that season?

Not all moments in our lives can be revisited with joy. However, in looking back over difficult episodes, I want to share an important truth God has taught me. He always uses everything we go through and works them together for good (Romans 8:28). Do you remember the story of Joseph? He had been mistreated by his family, sold into slavery, and falsely accused of a crime. Yet, through it all, he remained faithful to God. In the end, when he was reunited with the very individuals who had mistreated him, He communicated a profound truth.

> **"As for you, you meant evil against me, but God meant it for good in order to bring about this present result, to preserve many people alive." (Genesis 50:20)**

Joseph viewed his circumstances through the lens of God's character and, therefore, was able to forgive and even help those who had caused him harm. Even though the enemy uses tactics to come against us, God will use the same circumstances as tools to help grow us.

In days to come, we will dive deeper into the significance of remembering special seasons where God did a great work. Periods where transformation takes place, and lessons learned will never be forgotten. Times where God does a final work, in and through a situation in your life, before moving you forward to your next assignment. Treasure your Gilgal moments as well as special seasons that God will take you through. They will always be a part of our journey.

Day 2: Remember

I was losing hope. I had prayed earnestly for God to intervene in my situation. Yet, as time went by, my circumstances remained the same. With my limited vision, I could not see any movement on God's part. Yet even though my faith was weak, God's faithfulness remained strong. Little did I know that at the moment of my greatest crisis, the Lord was orchestrating a miracle I could never have imagined. In spite of how everything looked, God was ever-present in my circumstances. God worked. The miracle came, and to this day, I remember it.

During moments of uncertainty, it always helps to look back to what God has done in the past. Through periods of our own lives, as well as through instances recorded in His Word, we can trace

God's hand at work. In recalling such times, we are reminded of the Lord's faithfulness to His promises and to His children.

Read Mark 8:1-21.

> **According to verses 2–3, how was Jesus affected?**
>
>
> **According to verse 4, what question did the disciples ask Jesus? What concern held their attention?**

The disciples were focusing more on the impossibility of their situation instead of on Jesus. They had given more credence to what they "could not see" as a result of their lack of faith, instead of to what Jesus could do through His miraculous power.

Read verse 5 once more:

> **And He was asking them, "How many loaves do you have?" And they said, "Seven."**

So often we come to Jesus with our eyes fixed on what we do not have instead of on what He has to offer. We long to see before we decide to believe, but that is not faith. Second Corinthians 5:7 states, "For we walk by faith, not by sight."

> **How does this scripture passage speak to you with regard to your faith?**

In spite of the disciples' unbelief, Jesus was setting the stage for a miracle. He took what was placed before Him and multiplied it.

> **According to verse 8, how many baskets of food were left over?**

After performing the miracle, Jesus entered the boat with His disciples. Then the Bible states, "they embarked to the other side." Yet no sooner had they departed when another crisis of belief arose.

> **According to verse 14, what was the situation with regard to their food supply? What matter occupied the disciples' thoughts?**

Notice the following words of Jesus in response to His disciples' lack of faith (Mark 8:17-21):

And Jesus, aware of this, said to them, "Why do you discuss the fact that you have no bread? Do you not yet see or understand? Do you have a hardened heart? HAVING EYES, DO YOU NOT SEE? AND HAVING EARS, DO YOU NOT HEAR? And do you not remember, when I broke the five loaves for the five thousand, how many baskets full of broken pieces you picked up?" They said to Him, "Twelve." "When I broke the seven for the four thousand, how many large baskets full of broken pieces did you pick up?" And they said to Him, "Seven." And He was saying to them, "Do you not yet understand?"

What was Jesus teaching His disciples?

Go back and underline in verse 18, "And do you not remember." Jesus was reminding His disciples of the miracle He had just performed. In other words, Jesus had always come through. So why worry presently? Not a lot of time had elapsed since the feeding of the four thousand. Jesus was calling His disciples to believe by encouraging them to remember.

How can remembering past victories cause you to hope in the midst of current trials?

After the children of Israel arrived in Gilgal, the Lord called them to take a particular action, one that would remind them of what He had done during their journey. The Israelites were instructed "to remember." Read Joshua 4:1-13.

According to verses 2–3, what instructions did the Lord give Joshua?

What was the purpose of the twelve stones, according to verses 6–7?

The children of Israel obeyed God's commands. They took up the twelve stones as they were directed and placed them in a particular area where those stones would act as a visible reminder of God's faithfulness in bringing them to the Promised Land.

It is always good to look back on God's faithfulness and remember. For years, I listened to people talk about keeping journals where they recorded specific accounts of God's action on their behalf. One day, I decided to try it for myself. Now, many years later, with a closet full of journals, I often find myself looking back on how the Lord intervened during numerous trials. Each entry is a handwritten memorial of God's devotion, and these memorial stones fill the countless pages of many journals.

As we close today, join me in laying a few memorial stones to mark God's faithfulness in your own life.

My Personal Memorial Stones (a few of many)

- Rearing children without an earthly dad.

- A time when individuals were coming against one of my family members, God gave me a personal word that He would protect my relative. He came through, just as He had spoken.

- A period when I was called to engage in doctoral studies and God provided the income.

- A time when God healed my heart from seasons of deep hurt.

Your Memorial Stones

As we close today, please take a few moments and add your own memorial stones. Together, let us remember the times where God intervened in the midst of difficult trials.

-

-

-

-

End with a thanksgiving prayer to God for His faithfulness.

Day 3: Recall

I can still picture the scene to this day. I was sitting on the floor with my three- and four-year-old children, holding stuffed figures. I was acting out a Bible story for my sweet babies, while using some of their toys to communicate the message. I will never forget their excitement and eagerness as I shared the story of Abraham.

I continued their spiritual training for years, but of course the methods changed as they matured. I desperately wanted to pour the Word of God into Randy and Mandy's lives, so we spent time doing various Bible studies, devotionals, and scripture memorizing together. To this day, my adult children can still quote particular scripture passages they learned when they were younger.

One of the greatest mission fields for single moms is their children. God calls us to meditate on His Word, to live our lives according to His truth, and to teach His Word to those He has entrusted to us.

In the book, *Courageous*, Robert Jeffress states, "If you are a parent, your most important task is not to raise your kids' SAT scores, get them into a good college, or develop them into star athletes. Your most important job as a parent is to teach your children what it means to love, follow, and obey Jesus Christ."[15]

Remember how Moses led the children of Israel toward the Promised Land. After his death, Joshua took his place. Yet, before Moses died, he commanded the Israelites to obey the Word of God and to teach their children to do the same. Read Deuteronomy 11:18-21:

---

15 Robert Jeffress, *Courageous: 10 Strategies for Thriving in a Hostile World* (Grand Rapids: Baker Books Publishing, 2020), 190. Used with permission.

You shall therefore impress these words of mine on your heart and on your soul; and you shall bind them as a sign on your hand, and they shall be as frontals on your forehead. You shall teach them to your sons, talking of them when you sit in your house and when you walk along the road and when you lie down and when you rise up. You shall write them on the doorposts of your house and on your gates, so that your days and the days of your sons may be multiplied on the land which the LORD swore to your fathers to give them, as long as the heavens remain above the earth.

> **Take a few moments to write out verse 18. Afterwards, share how you can personally apply this passage of scripture to your life.**
>
>
>
> **According to verse 19, what instruction was given to the Israelites?**

Now, let us pick back up today with the Israelites' journey under Joshua's leadership. Read Joshua 4:14-24.

> **According to verse 14, what did God do for Joshua?**

God is the one who gives favor. It is not something we attempt to earn on our own, or even can for that matter. Favor is always given by God for His glory. Joshua had been faithful to His Lord, and in front of all the people he had been leading, God honored him.

The Lord had performed a miracle by causing the water to rise up so that His children could cross over on dry ground.

> **According to verses 17–18, what additional action did the Lord take on behalf of the Israelites?**
>
>
>
> **Where were the children of Israel camping at this particular point in their journeys?**
>
>
>
> **According to verse 20, where were the twelve memorial stones discovered?**

> **Where did Joshua put them?**

God wanted the children of Israel to recall His faithfulness, so Gilgal was chosen as the location for the memorial stones. Reread verses 20–24:

> **Those twelve stones which they had taken from the Jordan, Joshua set up at Gilgal. He said to the sons of Israel, "When your children ask their fathers in time to come, saying, 'What are these stones?' then you shall inform your children, saying, 'Israel crossed this Jordan on dry ground.' For the LORD your God dried up the waters of the Jordan before you until you had crossed, just as the LORD your God had done to the Red Sea, which He dried up before us until we had crossed; that all the peoples of the earth may know that the hand of the LORD is mighty, so that you may fear the LORD your God forever."**

Go back and underline in verse 21, "When your children ask." Moms, if we do not instruct our children in the ways of the Lord at home, someone else outside the home will direct them to the ways of the world. Go back and circle, in verse 22, "then you shall inform your children."

I remember meeting a young man in a store while I was attempting to share the gospel. He was so humble and very kind. However, I will never forget his response to me. After I asked if he was a Christian, he stated, "My parents never went to church, and I don't really know anything about it." Thankfully, through the Lord's ongoing work in the young man's heart, he became a Christian a few months later.

Here are a few suggestions for investing in your children's and grandchildren's lives:

1. Ask the Lord to lead you and your children to a church. Make church attendance a must in your family, not a casual occurrence.

2. Allow your children to participate in Bible studies, mission trips, and children and youth functions.

3. Teach your children the Word of God at home. How? Have daily devotions. Choose a book of the Bible to go through with your children. Have times where you sit down and discuss what you have been studying.

4. Teach your children how to build their lives upon God's Word and how to apply His teachings to their daily living.

5. Engage in scripture memory. Give your children one passage of scripture a week to memorize. Talk about the truth of the passage and how they can apply it to their lives.

   Memorizing scripture will transform a heart as well as a mind. In the book, *Counseling the Hard Cases*, the author states the following:

   Scripture memory is a sharp, shining weapon against temptation. Memorizing Scripture invokes the aid of the Holy Spirit—God-on-the-scene in our struggles. The Spirit who dwells within us has the power to strengthen and comfort and gladden our hearts with his Word. The psalmist says in Ps 119:11, "I have treasured Your word in my heart so that I may not sin against You." By the power of the Holy Spirit working through the Word, we are set free from the slavery of our sinful nature (Rom 8:2, 10-11; 2 Cor 3:17), we are convicted of any hidden sin (Ps 19:12), we abound in the fruit of the Spirit (Gal 5:22-23), and we abound with hope (Rom 15:13)![16]

6. Talk about your own personal memorial stones with your children. Choose a special memory to share with your kids, either weekly or bi-weekly, where God intervened or answered particular prayers. Take them on a journey with you and with God.

7. Set the example. Let your children see you reading the Word of God, as well as living it out. Pray in front of your children, for your children, and for their special requests.

8. Worship. Dr. Deron Biles states the following as it relates to worship: "Worship is not something we attend; it is something that we do. Worship is attitudes and actions offered in service and submission to God. The attitudes we offer in submission to God may include love, honor, fear, praise, humility, reverence, and the fruit of the Spirit. Actions we offer in service to God may include Bible study, prayer, obedience to His Word, preaching, teaching, serving, listening, witnessing, singing, and meditating. What are components of a worship service? Every worship service is unique but exists for the primary purpose of bringing glory to God. Worship services will be unique depending on the context or occasion. They generally include most or all of the following: prayer, reading of scripture, music (congregational singing, special music, etc.), ordinances, offering, sermon, response, and benediction."[17]

Special note: If these practices are new to you, ask the Lord to help you understand how to best minister to your children and teach them His Word. Find a godly woman in your church to help instruct you in the ways of the Lord, in His Word, and in teaching your children.

> **What memorial stones can you introduce your children to today?**

Memorial stones when I was younger: Discuss with your children how God brought you through difficult times at school.

Memorial stones during times of crises: Discuss how God intervened during a tough trial in your life while you were a child, a teenager, or even now as an adult (be age-appropriate of course).

Memorial stones about the importance of prayer: Discuss periods where God answered your prayers with a "yes," as well as times where God said "no" for a greater purpose.

A great harvest can come from speaking out about what the Lord has done in our lives. Look once more at verse 24:

> **"That all the peoples of the earth may know that the hand of the LORD is mighty, so that you may fear the LORD your God forever."**

Moms, let us stand strong and be determined to invest the Word of God in our children's lives. Always teach them His truth. Let them see His love, His forgiveness, His mercy, and His faithfulness through you. The harvest will be great and the blessings many.

---

16 Stuart Scott and Health Lambert, *Counseling the Hard Cases* (Nashville: B&H, 2012), 129. Used with permission.

17 D. Deron Biles, Professor of Preaching and Pastoral Ministry at Southwestern Baptist Theological Seminary. Written for *Strong and Courageous* Launch Series. Used with permission.

Day 4: Rest

I remember serving with a wonderful ministry which I greatly enjoyed. Yet as time went by, God was calling me to travel a different path. I was excited over the new opportunity and looked forward with anticipation to its beginning. However, in the midst of the transition, enemies began to surface—people whom I had known for years and had even counted as friends. During this difficult season, God kept me close underneath His wings, protecting me through it all.

Enemies: They exist. They may show up in the midst of our successes, attempting to stop what the Lord has called us to do. They may show up during our failures, endeavoring to kick us while we are down. They often lurk behind corners in deceptive ways as they attempt to devour their prey.

To our faces, they are kind; yet behind our backs, they are vicious. When they attack, they come with a vengeance. They seek to destroy people's lives while inflicting pain. Yet, despite their destructiveness, one thing is sure. They will never be allowed to engage in any more than what the Lord permits.

Jehoshaphat was a man God used mightily. On one particular occasion, as the enemies approached his camp, he found himself crying out to the only one who could save him.

Read 2 Chronicles 20:1-19.

According to verse 2, what message was reported to Jehoshaphat?

According to verse 3, what emotion did Jehoshaphat experience? What action did he take in response to the news he heard?

According to verse 4, how did the people choose to handle the threat from their enemies?

Glance back over the prayer of Jehoshaphat (vv. 5–11). Notice his pattern of supplication.

First, he reminded God of who He is. Second, he recalled all the Lord had done for the children of Israel. Third, he acknowledged the Lord's power.

After Jehoshaphat poured his heart out to God, he then made a stunning plea. Take a few moments to ponder verse 12:

> "O our God, will You not judge them? For we are powerless before this great multitude who are coming against us; nor do we know what to do, but our eyes are on You."

What question did he bring to God in verse 12?

Notice two important truths which he communicated to the Lord: "We are powerless," and "we don't know what to do." To have stopped with just those two declarations would have been so easy. Yet, the man of God knew who was in control of His situation. Therefore, his focus quickly shifted from the trial at-hand to the God above. He ended his prayer by declaring, "But our eyes are on You."

Woman of God, no matter what or who comes at you, God is in control of the situation. If you feel powerless before your enemies or lack wisdom about what to do, you must immediately choose to put your eyes on the One who can intervene in your situation.

Note: A good rule of thumb here is to always remember previous moments where God intervened on your behalf. It always helps to remember God's faithfulness in past victories.

As Jehoshaphat finished his prayer, everyone committed to a time of waiting. Notice verse 13:

> **All Judah was standing before the LORD, with their infants, their wives and their children.**

Everyone was eager to hear from God and to see what He would do. In the midst of waiting, God spoke.

Reread verses 14–17. Notice God's response to His children's prayer.

- Do not fear or be dismayed (because of this great multitude).
- For the battle is not yours but God's.
- Go out and meet them.
- You need not fight in this battle.
- Station yourselves.
- Stand and see the salvation of the Lord (on your behalf).
- Do not fear or be dismayed (repeated here).
- Go out to face them (for the LORD is with you).

After hearing God's Word spoken, Jehoshaphat was confident of their success. How did he respond to what the Lord had promised? Read verses 18–19:

> **Jehoshaphat bowed his head with his face to the ground, and all Judah and the inhabitants of Jerusalem fell down before the LORD, worshiping the LORD. The Levites, from the sons of the Kohathites and of the sons of the Korahites, stood up to praise the LORD God of Israel, with a very loud voice. (2 Chronicles 20:18-19)**

> **How would you summarize Jehoshaphat's response to God's intervention?**

In closing, let us pick back up with the story of Joshua and the children of Israel. Remember, they were in Gilgal. The city of Jericho, which blocked the remaining entrance to the Promised Land, was located miles away. Even though the city was a place surrounded by walls and filled with enemies, it had to be captured. However, the victory was already theirs. While the hearts of the children of Israel were elated, the hearts of their enemies melted with fear.

Read Joshua 5:1:

> **Now it came about when all the kings of the Amorites who were beyond the Jordan to the west, and all the kings of the Canaanites who were by the sea, heard how**

the LORD had dried up the waters of the Jordan before the sons of Israel until they had crossed, that their hearts melted, and there was no spirit in them any longer because of the sons of Israel.

God worked as the Israelites continued to move forward. They could rest in the knowledge that He was in complete control of their adversaries. He knew their location, their plots, and their hearts' conditions. Notice once more how the kings of both the Amorites and Canaanites feared the Israelites. Go back and underline, "There was no spirit in them any longer because of the sons of Israel."

God had intervened in the lives of those determined to stop the Israelites from entering the land of promise. And my friend, He will do the same for you.

No enemy, no threat, and no barrier will ever interfere with the Lord's plans. Read the following scripture passages:

I know that You can do all things, And that no purpose of Yours can be thwarted. (Job 42:2)

"No weapon that is formed against you will prosper; And every tongue that accuses you in judgment you will condemn. This is the heritage of the servants of the LORD, And their vindication is from Me," declares the LORD. (Isaiah 54:17)

How do these passages give you confidence?

God is all-powerful and no match for those who come against His children. He will prevail. He will protect. He will act. God can deal with our enemies much more effectively than we can. The question is, will we trust Him to do just that? Rest.

Day 5: Repositioned

In our Gilgals, as well as in other places (or seasons) in which we may find ourselves residing, there will be various factors influencing our experiences. Moments will occur when healing needs to take place in our lives. Times will happen when the Lord steps on the scene to roll away the reproach of our past. God will provide periods where we can acknowledge His goodness with praise and thanksgiving. In these seasons, we will be provisioned and repositioned for the next stage of our journeys with changed hearts and renewed minds.

Let us revisit the children of Israel as we bring this week's lesson to a close. We will glean additional wisdom from the Israelites during their stay in Gilgal.

Read Joshua 5:2-9:

At that time, the LORD said to Joshua, "Make for yourself flint knives and circumcise again the sons of Israel the second time." So Joshua made himself flint knives and circumcised the sons of Israel at Gibeath-haaraloth. This is the reason why Joshua circumcised them: all the people who came out of Egypt who were males, all the men of war, died in the wilderness along the way after they came out of Egypt. For all the people who came out were circumcised, but all the people who were born in the wilderness along the way as they came out of Egypt had not been circumcised. For the sons of Israel walked forty years in the wilderness, until all the nation, that is, the men of war who came out of Egypt, perished because they did not listen to the voice of the LORD, to whom the LORD had sworn that He would not let them see the land which the LORD had sworn to their fathers to give us, a land flowing with milk and honey. Their children whom He raised up in their place, Joshua circumcised; for they were uncircumcised, because they had not circumcised them along the way. Now when they had finished circumcising all the nation, they remained in their places in the camp until they were healed. Then the LORD said to Joshua, "Today I have rolled away the reproach of Egypt from you." So the name of that place is called Gilgal to this day.

Remain (until healed)

According to verse 2, what instructions did the Lord give Joshua?

According to verse 8, what actions were taken by those who had been circumcised?

A time of healing had to take place before the children of Israel could move forward. Yet even though the healing in this passage refers to the healing following circumcision, the same truth holds true for us today with regard to our healing.

I remember the Lord speaking to me as if it were yesterday. I had crossed a line that had dishonored God, as well as many others. The devastation that followed included broken hearts. I had hurt the Lord and tainted my testimony. However, after I repented, God met me where I was and began a work of restoration I never thought possible.

Although the consequences of past sin were still real, I had been forgiven and restored to a right relationship with the Lord. I was ready to tell the world about my Savior and His restoring power. Though I had been forgiven, I had a heart that needed a lot of work, which included mending from past hurts and a sinful lifestyle. With the Lord, forgiveness was instant. However, complete healing would take much longer.

I was in my car one day when the Lord spoke clearly to me. God was using me and my testimony of restoration. Yet, I longed to be used in a greater way. As I was praying and talking to God about all I wanted to do, He quietly said in my spirit, *You're not ready yet.* It would be years before I would fully understand what He was saying. I eventually found myself in a Gilgal of my own. Gilgal became my time of healing and renewal.

Read Joshua 5:9:

Then the LORD said to Joshua, "Today I have rolled away the reproach of Egypt from you." So the name of that place is called Gilgal to this day.

Reproach (of Egypt) Rolled Away

Read Joshua 5:10:

> **While the sons of Israel camped at Gilgal they observed the Passover on the evening of the fourteenth day of the month on the desert plains of Jericho.**

Recognition (of the Lord's goodness)

Read Joshua 5:11-12:

> **On the day after the Passover, on that very day, they ate some of the produce of the land, unleavened cakes and parched grain. The manna ceased on the day after they had eaten some of the produce of the land, so that the sons of Israel no longer had manna, but they ate some of the yield of the land of Canaan during that year.**

Repositioned (in their journey)

During my time at seminary, I was blessed to be sponsored by an individual who believed in me and the calling God had placed upon my life. In seminary, this was my manna. While most students were working several different jobs to pay their way through school, I was afforded the opportunity to be a full-time student. When I graduated with my master's degree, this particular blessing would cease for a time, while God provided an entirely different avenue for income. I was now in my Promised Land and responsible to obtain the bread provided by God through different means.

The children of Israel had been taught many lessons during their stay in Gilgal. And, my sister, so will you and I. As stated previously, throughout our journeys, we will be called to our own camp Gilgals as well as to various seasons that will forever hold special places in our hearts. Remember the impact those periods can have and the influence that will come from the Master's teachings. Instead of dreading such moments, let us lift our hearts in praise and thanksgiving for God's appointed paths that bring us to such places.

For God is in control of our journeys. He knows exactly where we need to be in order to learn all we need to learn. Let us hold fast to His hand as He moves us closer to our Promised Land. May we remember God's faithfulness, His past victories, and always, His special promises. Remember His call to remember and to recall to others what He has taught you.

Notes

_____

_____

_____

_____

_____

_____

Week 6

The Call to Trust

~Check with your instructor about when to view this week's video.

During Week 6, we will address the following subject matters, focusing on biblical truths which give direction to our lives:

Day 1: "Obstacles" will instruct single moms to look at obstacles as opportunities instead of as disappointments or even blocks to their destinies.

Day 2: "Looking at Our Jerichos" will both instruct and encourage the ladies in the area of faith as they stand before their own personal Jerichos, instead of allowing such periods to birth fear and retreat.

Day 3: "I Have Come!" will encourage single moms to view their heavenly Father as One who rules over their journeys, instead of as One assisting them in their voyages.

Day 4: "The Battle Is the Lord's" will teach the ladies truths about allowing God to fight their battles. Single moms will be instructed to cease putting together their own battle plans.

Day 5: "Trust in the Lord" will impart truths to single moms about the importance of trusting God in and through their journeys. They will be reminded that God is a good Father and completely trustworthy.

Day 1: Obstacles

The ministry that provided numerous avenues of service for others was wonderful. I was elated over the opportunity to work with such an agency and looked forward to pouring myself into the work of that ministry. However, in the midst of this new beginning came attacks from individuals who did not believe in me—people who took it upon themselves to try and discourage others from giving me a chance at the particular job I had been asked to do. Their opposition turned into opportunities for not only my growth in Christ but also for God to show Himself mighty on behalf of His ministry as well as His child.

Obstacles will always be present in our journeys, ones that appear impossible to move and difficult to conquer. The enemy uses such barriers to attempt to block our way to our Promised Land. However, as we allow the Spirit of God to change our focus, we will learn how such obstacles can be viewed as opportunities, when He uses them for His glory and our own personal growth. Remember, nothing or no one has the power to stop what God has ordained.

Peter was a man used powerfully by God. Yet in his journey, he often faced insurmountable obstacles. On one particular occasion, the disciple had been arrested and placed in prison. As people gathered to pray for God to bring Peter out of prison, not only did God show up on Peter's behalf but He also moved obstacles that appeared unmovable.

Read Acts 12:1-17.

According to this passage, who arrested Peter, and why did they take such an action?

How many soldiers were commanded to guard Peter?

Who was praying for Peter's release?

Things probably looked very bleak for the disciple. Yet God was working on Peter's behalf even though he could not see it at the time.

According to verse 6, between how many soldiers was Peter sleeping? With what was he bound? Where were other guards located?

What miracle took place, according to verse 7?

> **What message did the angel bring to Peter? What happened to his chains?**

Glance back at verse 10:

> When they had passed the first and second guard, they came to the iron gate that leads into the city, which opened for them by itself; and they went out and went along one street, and immediately the angel departed from him.

> **How did the iron gate open?**

> **Take a few moments to list all the obstacles preventing Peter's escape from the prison cell. From a human standpoint, would you have said his escape was possible or impossible?**

> **How did God use the barriers in Peter's path to grow him as well as those who were praying for him?**

> **How did God's intervention glorify Himself?**

At first, Peter thought he was seeing a vision. Yet, later, he realized more was going on than he had originally perceived. Reread verse 11:

> When Peter came to himself, he said, "Now I know for sure that the Lord has sent forth His angel and rescued me from the hand of Herod and from all that the Jewish people were expecting."

Go back and underline, "<u>Now I know</u>." The miraculous delivery increased Peter's faith in His Lord. He recognized that God was the one who had orchestrated his escape. No human could have done what God did. While the believers expected one outcome, God brought about an entirely different one.

When Peter arrived at the place where the church had gathered to pray, he knocked on the door. A young woman named Rhoda answered. Yet, the minute she saw it was Peter, she ran to tell everyone the news and neglected to let him enter. Unfortunately, her hearers did not believe it was really Peter. They had been praying for God to intervene, yet when He did, they gave more credence to their doubts than to God's ability to answer their prayers.

I remember a lady standing before a group of women at a retreat while sharing her testimony about the return of a prodigal son. Week after week, women joined together to pray for the young man who had wandered away from God. One day, to the mother's surprise, a lady reached out to share some great news. She told the mother that her son had been in church the night before. Immediately, the mother responded, "What was he doing there?" She had asked God to bring him back, yet when God answered, she was in utter shock.

Listen, there is nothing that God cannot handle.

> **Have you ever allowed an obstacle in your life to obscure your vision, dream, or calling?**

In closing, let us revisit some scenes in the Bible where obstacles made hope seem impossible, yet God's power provided an entirely different outcome:

People Involved: **Abraham and Sarah (Genesis 18)**

Situation: **Abraham and Sarah were promised a child.**

The Obstacle: **Sarah was barren and well-advanced in age.**

Sarah's Response: **Sarah laughed at the possibility of having a child in her old age (v. 12).**

God's Response: **"Is anything too difficult for the Lord?" (v. 14).**

End Result: **God brought forth what He had promised: a baby.**

***

People Involved: **A father and son (Mark 9:14-29)**

Situation: **The father was attempting to obtain help for his son who was demon possessed.**

The Obstacle: **Unbelief in the Lord's ability to intervene.**

The Man's Question: **"But if You can do anything, take pity on us and help us!" (v. 22).**

Jesus' Response: **"If you can? All things are possible to the one who believes" (v. 23).**

End Result: **Jesus cast out the demon.**

***

People Involved: **A sick man and Jesus (John 5:1-9)**

Situation: **The man had been ill for thirty-eight years (v. 5).**

The Obstacle: **The sick man was always blocked from getting to the healing waters.**

Jesus' Question: **"Do you wish to get well?" (v. 6).**

The Sick Man's Response: **"Sir, I have no man to put me into the pool when the water is stirred up, but while I am coming, another steps down before me"** (v. 7).

End Result: **Jesus intervened and brought healing to the man.**

Let us take a few moments to look at an example of my own obstacle chart.

People Involved: **Me**

Situation: **Joblessness**

The Obstacle: **Continued blocks on jobs for which I was applying.**

My Question: **"God, what is going on?"**

God's Response: **"Wait."**

End Result: **The best job I had ever been offered came. The blocks that I saw as obstacles were actually God's blockades used to keep me from going to the wrong places in order to bring me to the job He had ordained for me.**

What about you? Take a few moments to fill in your own personal obstacle chart. What has God revealed to you about your blockade?

People Involved:

Situation:

The Obstacle:

My Question:

God's Response:

Remember, obstacles are merely opportunities for God to work. Ask the Lord to give you His perspective on your obstacle.

Day 2: Looking at Our Jericho

It is a time that all Christians will have to face. It is a period that will call for incredible faith. It is a moment that will be remembered for years to come. It is a location where many will indeed stand. To what am I referring?

Jericho: A situation deemed as an obstacle, blocking the entrance to our Promised Lands. A post or station that must be conquered as we move toward our inheritance. A few examples, out of many, of our own personal Jerichos can be *thoughts* (attempting to block our view of the promised miracle), *enemies* (endeavoring to stop God's plans), *emotions of unbelief* and *fear* (seeking to persuade God's children to give up and doubt His ability to come through), or *places* we have been called to inhabit though surrounded by walls of adversity.

Jericho was stationed in a section of the Promised Land, though blocking the remaining entrance to the children of Israel's inheritance. While stationed at Gilgal, Joshua and the Israelites viewed Jericho from afar. When they saw the high walls surrounding the city, anxiety probably seized their hearts as they wondered how they might take the fortified city. The barriers seemed enormous. However, this was not the first time Joshua had faced obstacles. Years before, while under the leadership of Moses, the children of Israel found themselves facing obstructions that seemed unmovable. Let us take a few minutes to look back at a pivotal time in Israel's history.

Read Numbers 13:1-2:

> **Then the LORD spoke to Moses saying, "Send out for yourself men so that they may spy out the land of Canaan, which I am going to give to the sons of Israel; you shall send a man from each of their fathers' tribes, everyone a leader among them."**

God had promised the land of Canaan to the children of Israel. As they prepared to inherit this promise, Moses sent twelve spies to examine the terrain. Going in, they were probably filled with a sense of confident expectation. Yet when they came out, it would be a different story. Ten would return bearing a negative report, while two others would arrive with an entirely different description of the land. Guess who one of those two was? Joshua.

Read Numbers 13:25-33.

Let us take a few minutes to examine the report given by the ten spies versus the report given by the two faithful men, Caleb and Joshua.

Report of the Ten

> **Thus they told him, and said, "We went in to the land where you sent us; and it certainly does flow with milk and honey, and this is its fruit. Nevertheless, the people who live in the land are strong, and the cities are fortified and *very large*; and moreover, we saw the descendants of Anak there." (vv. 27–28)**

The first part of the spies' report assured the people of the land's productivity. It contained all that God had promised. However, the second portion of their description would give more credence to the obstacles in the land than to what God had spoken.

Their response to the obstacles revealed the true condition of their hearts. Go back and underline, "Nevertheless." This word communicated a message that would cause many hearts to fear. What were they actually saying? "The land is all that God said it was, but 'nevertheless,' it will be impossible to take."

Report of the Two (Caleb and Joshua)

> **Then Caleb quieted the people before Moses and said, "We should by all means go up and take possession of it, for we will surely overcome it." (v. 30)**

Response of the Ten

"We are not able to go up against the people, for they are too strong for us." (v. 31)

Caleb stepped up to calm the people and to encourage them. In time, both Moses and Joshua would join him in this endeavor. The hearts of Caleb and Joshua were different than the other ten spies. They believed God in spite of any obstacles standing in their way. Yes, the land had giants, but God was bigger. Yes, it seemed impossible, but they knew that with God, nothing was impossible. While their report articulated hope and faith, the other spies communicated an entirely different message.

Take a look at Numbers 14:1-2:

> **Then all the congregation lifted up their voices and cried, and the people wept that night. All the sons of Israel grumbled against Moses and Aaron; and the whole congregation said to them, "Would that we had died in the land of Egypt! Or would that we had died in this wilderness!"**

> **According to this passage, what was the response of the children of Israel to the bad report? How had their focus shifted?**

Read Numbers 14:5-8.

Caleb and Joshua believed they could enter the land. Why? Because they chose to believe God. Furthermore, as a result of their obedience, they would later be allowed to enter the Promised Land. The ten spies, however, would never see it.

Many years later, Joshua would once again find himself surveying a section of land that awaited his conquest. This land included a city encircled with numerous barriers. The city? Jericho.

Read Joshua 5:13:

> **Now it came about when Joshua was by Jericho, that he lifted up his eyes and looked, and behold, a man was standing opposite him with his sword drawn in his hand, and Joshua went to him and said to him, "Are you for us or for our adversaries?"**

Go back and underline the first part of verse 13, "<u>Now it came about when Joshua was by Jericho.</u>"

As Joshua glared at the fortified city, he knew the time was drawing near to conquer the land. Had the leader slipped away from the children of Israel to glance at the city alone? Did he go away to seek God's counsel as he wondered how those walls would come down? All of these scenarios could be true. However, we do know that he was standing by Jericho.

> **Can you recall a time when you were standing before your own personal Jericho? Was it a place that looked impossible to overtake? Were you facing a trial that appeared too great for you to bear? Take a moment to write it down.**

As Joshua surveyed his Jericho, he was met by a visitor who would change not only his thought process but his vision as well. It would be a visitation he would never forget.

No matter where we currently find ourselves, we must allow the Lord to shift our focus onto Him instead of on the circumstances at hand. Colossians 3:2 says,

> **Set your mind on the things above, not on the things that are on earth.**

Focus matters. Put your eyes on Jesus, and let Him take care of the barrier that is begging for your attention. He's got your Jericho!

Day 3: I Have Come!

There it was! A hurdle larger than any words could describe. An obstruction that looked immovable. A Promised Land I so desperately wanted to inherit was blocked by what appeared to be an impossible barrier. Had I not heard correctly from God?

A battle raged in my mind. On one hand, I felt I had received a message from God with regard to where He was leading me. Yet by contrast, the circumstances seemed to point in a different direction. Though a human perspective was one of hopelessness, God's Word conveyed a message of assurance.

In a moment's time, God spoke to my heart, reminding me of His character and a very important truth. He was the One over my Jericho as well as my voyage ahead. His revelation would forever change the way I looked not only at my Jericho but my entire journey as well.

Read Joshua 5:13-15:

> **Now it came about when Joshua was by Jericho, that he lifted up his eyes and looked, and behold, a man was standing opposite him with his sword drawn in his hand, and Joshua went to him and said to him, "Are you for us or for our adversaries?" He said, "No; rather I indeed come now as captain of the host of the LORD." And Joshua fell on his face to the earth, and bowed down, and said to him, "What has my lord to say to his servant?" The captain of the LORD's host said to Joshua, "Remove your sandals from your feet, for the place where you are standing is holy." And Joshua did so.**

On a Sunday afternoon, as I read this particular passage, I was standing before my own Jericho. Before hearing God speak from the passage in Joshua, I had wondered how God might intervene. In other words, I was attempting to figure out how God could possibly bring down the walls which surrounded my Promised Land. Yet is not that always the case? We spend more time attempting to assist God than we do trusting Him.

I want to point you back to a period when Moses was leading the children of Israel. God had spoken a promise to his leader, and Moses was responsible to convey it to the Israelites. Yet, instead of trusting the Lord to bring it to fruition, Moses thought it was his responsibility to attempt to figure out what to do.

Read Numbers 11:16-23.

> **According to verse 18, what did the children of Israel crave at this particular point in their journey?**

Look back once more to what the Lord commanded Moses to say to the Israelites:

> "Therefore the LORD will give you meat and you shall eat."

> **How long did the Lord promise to give them meat?**

Notice the questions which Moses posed to God, after hearing His promise to supply meat for the children of Israel:

> But Moses said, "The people, among whom I am, are 600,000 on foot; yet You have said, 'I will give them meat, so that they may eat for a whole month.' Should flocks and herds be slaughtered for them, to be sufficient for them? Or should all the fish of the sea be gathered together for them, to be sufficient for them?" (Numbers 11:21-22)

Moses had taken it upon himself to attempt to bring about God's promise. He suggested several possibilities to the Lord. Yet, notice God's answer in verse 23:

> The LORD said to Moses, "Is the LORD's power limited? Now you shall see whether My word will come true for you or not."

Read Numbers 11:31-32.

> **According to these verses, did the Lord fulfill His promise? Did He need Moses' help to accomplish His task?**
>
> **Has there ever been a time in your life when you attempted to "fix" a situation instead of allowing God to handle it? If so, what happened as a result?**

Let us pick back up with Joshua 5:13-14:

> Now it came about when Joshua was by Jericho, that he lifted up his eyes and looked, and behold, a man was standing opposite him with his sword drawn in his hand, and Joshua went to him and said to him, "Are you for us or for our adversaries?" He said, "No; rather I indeed come now as captain of the host of the

Lord." And Joshua fell on his face to the earth, and bowed down, and said to him, "What has my lord to say to his servant?"

I want you to go back and underline, "I indeed come now as captain of the host of the Lord."

God Himself had appeared to Joshua. He had stepped onto the scene to remind His servant that He had come to take Jericho. In other words, Jericho was not Joshua's responsibility; it was under the Lord's feet and firmly in His hands.

A particular season had been a struggle for me. Fear had gripped me, and my faith was weakening. How in the world would God come through? The situation looked impossible. Yet, after reading this passage of scripture, I took an entirely different view of my journey. I did not have to try and figure out what God wanted me to do. I did not have to plan how to take my Promised Land. God was in control, and He had come to remind me of this truth.

The Lord not only has our physical lives in His hands, but He also has our spiritual journeys under His control. He is *over* them, *in charge* of them, and *responsible* for them. We are simply to follow Him and be obedient to His call. Women of God, stop trying to figure everything out. The Lord has come! He stands ready to guide you on the journey He has called you to take. Rest in this truth.

Day 4: The Battle Is the Lord's

My phone rang one day, and a very disgruntled family member was on the other line. A trial had exposed anger within her heart. As I listened to her voice her concerns, sadness filled my soul. I was grieved over her trial. For a moment, my flesh wanted to fix the problem and intervene. However, I was reminded that the battle was not mine but the Lord's.

Battle plans are often drawn up by families, married couples, and individuals while facing a crisis. They are often formed without giving any thought to God's direction for trials. Instead, we decide how to handle these situations by leaning on our own understanding. We wring our hands over what to do next and stay up all night, fretting over imagined outcomes, ones which usually never come to fruition. However, when we take a moment to calm down and seek the Lord, we find that He is the One who is Captain over not only our journey but also the battle which is raging. A bowed knee before the throne of God is always better than any plan we can develop on our own.

As we discussed yesterday, Joshua was standing by Jericho when he was met by the Lord. Today, let us pick back up with Joshua 5:13-15:

> **Now it came about when Joshua was by Jericho, that he lifted up his eyes and looked, and behold, a man was standing opposite him with his sword drawn in his hand, and Joshua went to him and said to him, "Are you for us or for our adversaries?" He said, "No; rather I indeed come now as captain of the host of the Lord." And Joshua fell on his face to the earth, and bowed down, and said to him, "What has my lord to say to his servant?" The captain of the Lord's host said to Joshua, "Remove your sandals from your feet, for the place where you are standing is holy." And Joshua did so.**

I want you to notice something of great significance in verse 13.

> **"A man was standing opposite him with his sword drawn in his hand."**

Not only had the Lord stepped on the scene to help, but He had arrived prepared for battle.

John MacArthur commented, "The commander, sword drawn, showed a posture indicating He was set to give Israel victory over the Canaanites."[18]

> **Have you ever found yourself in the middle of a heated battle and God came to your defense? Share your story in the space provided.**

When we allow God to intervene on our behalf, He will accomplish more than we could have ever done on our own. He knows when to intervene and when to wait. He knows what needs removing and what needs to stay. He knows the course of action which needs to be taken. He sees what we do not. He protects us from unimagined danger.

I remember an individual in my life who I loved like a family member, but over time, God began to caution me in regard to this particular association. I overlooked those alerts and continued to move forward in the friendship. I later discovered that instead of having a trusted alliance, I was associating with an untrusted one. As I tried so desperately to remain friends, the Lord blocked my attempts until I was able to see and understand what He was protecting me from the entire time. God truly knows what He is doing.

At another time in my journey, I faced a dispute, and I made my own plans for what needed to be done to resolve it. Though God warned me to stop, I continued to advance forward. While others were counseling me to let God work, I continued working out my own plan. Later, I learned the hard way the importance of listening to the Lord and to godly counsel. After experiencing destruction and great hurt, my attitude changed in regard to fighting my own battles. Had I allowed the Lord to fight for me, the outcome would have been much different.

> **Are you currently facing a battle in your life? If so, who is in control of this conflict?**

Joshua was encouraged that God had come on behalf of the children of Israel. No matter what you and I are currently facing, we must remember this amazing truth. The Lord has come with His sword, His power, and His might. We do not have to worry about putting together a battle plan for situations we are facing. Let the Captain take charge. In the long run, you will be glad you did.

Day 5: Trust in the Lord

As we close this week's lesson, I will briefly review truths learned through Joshua's encounter with the Lord. As we have previously discussed, the Lord appeared to Joshua with a sword drawn, ready for battle. God wanted Joshua to know that He had come! He desired Joshua to know that He was in control. In addition, the Lord wanted Joshua to follow His lead in taking Jericho and to rest in the

---

18 MacArthur, *Unleashing God's Truth*, 260.

fact that He would. He was over Jericho, and He was over Joshua and the children of Israel. Simply put: God wanted Joshua to trust Him.

I remember a time when I too stood gazing at a particular Jericho. In my mind, I knew the Lord could handle it, take it, and do all that was needed to bring victory. Yet, in my heart, an entirely different desire was present. A secret battle was ensuing, one that was strangling my faith.

On the surface, I appeared to be a woman of great confidence. In fact, I often had people tell me, "You have so much faith." Yet, little did they know that faith was an area where I often experienced great defeat. I knew that nothing was too difficult for God, but I struggled to believe that He would do something great in my life.

As time went by, I found myself drowning in unbelief. I was doubting God more than ever. I prayed over and over about my Jericho but continued to overlook the persistent struggle within my own heart. Then the Lord revealed an important truth. He was more concerned about my unbelief than He was in conquering my Jericho. He was more interested in a relationship with me, while I only wanted Him for what He could do for me.

As I got to know the Lord, my trust grew, and through prayer and Bible study, my faith began to flourish. I had not realized how my lack of faith was hindering my walk, my journey, and my life.

Our trust is often hindered when we are worrying and fretting instead of seeking. Look at Psalm 46:10:

> **"Cease striving and know that I am God; I will be exalted among the nations, I will be exalted in the earth."**

According to this passage of scripture, what is God calling us to do?

Read Matthew 6:25-34.

According to these passages, what is God calling us to do?

Often our trust is hindered because we fear God will not help us or stand by us. Read Psalm 9:10:

> **And those who know Your name will put their trust in You, For You, O LORD, have not forsaken those who seek You.**

According to this passage of scripture, how is God's character described? How does knowing He will never forsake His own help you to trust Him more?

Read Joshua 1:9:

> **"Have I not commanded you? Be strong and courageous! Do not tremble or be dismayed, for the LORD your God is with you wherever you go."**

> **According to this passage of scripture, is God with us some of the time, or always?**

Look at Hebrews 13:8:

> Jesus Christ is the same yesterday and today and forever.

> **What assurance does this passage give us? How does this assurance help us to trust God?**

Our trust is often hindered because we wonder how in the world God will work out the mess we are in or in the trial that has come our way.

Read Romans 8:28:

> And we know that God causes all things to work together for good to those who love God, to those who are called according to His purpose.

> **How does knowing this truth help your trust?**
>
> **How important to God is our trusting Him and having faith in Him?**

Read Hebrews 11:6:

> And without faith it is impossible to please Him, for he who comes to God must believe that He is and that He is a rewarder of those who seek Him.

And without _____ it is _____ to _____ Him.

> **According to Psalm 37:5, we are told to do two things. What are they?**

> Commit your way to the LORD, Trust also in Him, and He will do it.

> **Does God say we walk by faith or by sight (2 Corinthians 5:7)?**

> **How would you describe your relationship with Jesus today? Would you say the number one desire in your life right now is to know Him, to love Him with all your heart, and to glorify Him? Or are you more concerned over what He can fix or take care of or over which He can give you victory?**

Listen, my desire in speaking these truths is not to condemn you. I just want to share some simple yet profound truths that I have learned. Let God set you apart to Himself. Let Him teach you who He is. Let Him have your fears, your doubts, your unbelief. Let Him conquer you before He conquers your Jericho. Get into His Word and get to know Him.

Is there anything hindering your trust in God? Unbelief? Unanswered prayers? Or maybe prayers answered in a different way than what you had hoped? If you are struggling in any one of these areas, or maybe in other areas that are affecting your trust, invite Jesus into those sections today and let Him speak His truth to you. Ask Him to help your unbelief (Mark 9:24).

God is a trustworthy God. We can trust Him in all things, with all things, and through all things—and we will always be called to do so. He stands ready to deliver, ready to conquer, and ready to move on our behalves. He has our Jerichos, our families, and our journeys, and He is over, in charge of, and working in and through them as we speak. You can trust Him—always!

Over the next several minutes, spend time with God in prayer, asking Him to help you trust Him more. Dive into His Word and get to know Him.

Notes

_____

_____

_____

_____

_____

_____

_____

_____

_____

_____

Week 7

The Call to Obey

~Check with your instructor about when to view this week's video.

During Week 7, we will address the following subject matters, focusing on biblical truths which give direction to our lives:

Day 1: "Say What?" will teach single moms biblical truths as they relate to God's directives for their lives even though the instructions may appear to go against human logic.

Day 2: "Obey God's Instructions" will impart truths to the ladies as to the importance of always obeying God's instructions.

Day 3: "Do Not Give Up" will encourage single moms as to the importance of never giving up in their journeys, no matter the difficulties that lie before them.

Day 4: "I Do Not See Anything Happening" will teach the importance of continuing to move forward according to God's Word and instructions, even though they may not see any hint of His working on their behalves.

Day 5: "The Walls Come Down" will close the study with a reminder for single moms that God reigns over their journeys and will bring down in complete victory those walls surrounding their Jerichos.

Day 1: Say What?

I remember a particular time in my journey when the Lord revealed a specific message about the situation I was facing. His directions were precise and right on time. However, to many, His instructions seemed unwise. Yet to me, the Lord's message lined up perfectly with what I believed He was getting ready to do in my life. Thus, even though His directives appeared risky to others, I knew with certainty it was the way I needed to go. I understood the importance of following His lead in my situation.

I have often been amazed at the dialogues I have encountered as Christians make decisions about life, jobs, and families from a worldly mindset.

I remember serving with a particular group of individuals in a ministry endeavor in which, at times, I would encounter thinking completely opposed to the Word of God. On several occasions, human logic was employed as the leadership attempted to run the ministry like a business instead of under the Lord's leadership.

In like manner, Joshua received directives that would oppose mortal reasoning. The Lord stepped onto the scene of the impending battle of Jericho, and Joshua was humbled and awestruck by the presence of God Himself. Yet, after the encounter, the Lord gave specific instructions to Joshua with regard to Jericho.

Let us pick up today with Joshua 6:1-5:

> **Now Jericho was tightly shut because of the sons of Israel; no one went out and no one came in. The Lord said to Joshua, "See, I have given Jericho into your hand, with its king and the valiant warriors. You shall march around the city, all the men of war circling the city once. You shall do so for six days. Also seven priests shall carry seven trumpets of rams' horns before the ark; then on the seventh day you shall march around the city seven times, and the priests shall blow the trumpets. It shall be that when they make a long blast with the ram's horn, and when you hear the sound of the trumpet, all the people shall shout with a great shout; and the wall of the city will fall down flat, and the people will go up every man straight ahead."**

According to verses 1 and 2, what impediments stood between Joshua and Jericho?

In spite of the hindrances facing the children of Israel, what assurance did God give Joshua?

What instructions did the Lord give to Joshua in reference to his conquest of Jericho? List the orders as bullet points. I will start for you.

- You shall march one time around the city for six days ("all the men of war").

-

-

-

-

-

If Joshua were alive today, and these instructions were given, how do you think people would respond to these kinds of directives?

God often works in mysterious ways. He approaches our situations in ways we find baffling, while calling us to take specific actions we may not understand. He calls us to wait when we think we should move forward. He calls us to step out in faith in response to His specific calling without an ability to see the entire picture, and always, He calls us to take Him at His Word even when our circumstances seem to contradict what He has said.

Look closely at the following examples from scripture:

Read 2 Kings 5:1-14.

How was Naaman regarded by the people?

What instructions were given to Naaman in order to be cured of leprosy?

How did Naaman first respond to the Lord's instructions?

> **What steps of obedience did he eventually take in order for his leprosy to be cured?**
>
>
> **Had Naaman been given the opportunity to write his story a different way, how do you think he might have told it?**

No matter how Naaman viewed his situation, he was impacted greatly by the way God intervened. After Naaman obeyed God's command, he came to a greater understanding of who God really was. After he was healed, he proclaimed,

"Behold now, I know that there is no God in all the earth, but in Israel." (v. 15)

Read Genesis 6:13-22.

> **According to verse 13, what message did God give to Noah?**
>
>
> **According to verse 17, how was God going to destroy the earth?**
>
>
> **What did God ask Noah to build?**
>
>
> **As Noah was given these instructions, was the Flood in sight?**

Whatever God tells you to do in any situation you are facing, take Him at His Word. If He tells you to move forward, go. If He tells you to go in a different direction, do it. If He tells you to step out in faith, do not hesitate to obey. Or if He gives you specific instructions about how to handle a matter, though it might not make sense to you, do it anyway.

We must stop expecting everything to make sense to us with regard to God's commands. Instead, we must learn to trust Him because of who He is. When we move forward in obedience, victory will surely be ours. Yet, when we attempt to live our lives according to the world's wisdom, we are destined for disappointment.

Joshua listened to the voice of God, obeyed Him, and moved according to God's direction. As his enemies lined the walls of Jericho, they probably made fun of the Israelites as they marched around it each day. However, their laughter and mockery did not stop the children of Israel from carrying out the Lord's command. We would do well to follow their example.

Day 2: Obey God's Instructions

At one particular point in my mother's journey, the Lord sent a message that transformed her life. It was a season marked by trials and hardship, a season that was quite devastating. Pain filled my mother's heart, while shame and discouragement threatened to overwhelm her soul. She was barely hanging on to her sanity and her strength.

One day, my mother returned to her office from lunch. As she walked through the doors of her business, she proceeded down a long hallway, while greeting those she met along the way. Before entering her department, she glanced over at the familiar face of a local pastor who was talking with an employee. She briefly said hello and continued to walk to her office. After arriving, she sat down at her desk and began to work. Soon she was interrupted by a knock on her door, and she received a message she never imagined nor anticipated.

The man at her door was the elderly pastor, well-loved and respected by those within his community. He walked over and stood at my mother's desk and proceeded to share a truth he had heard earlier that day from his heavenly Father. He stated, "The Lord told me I needed to talk to you." Though my mother sat speechless, she hung on every word spoken by the pastor. "Embrace Psalm 37, as you walk through this trial," he said. "God will see you through." He then turned around and walked away.

My mother learned later that the elderly gentleman had awakened on that particular morning and walked outside to have his prayer time with God. As he did, the Lord had impressed upon his heart a word of encouragement for my mother from Psalm 37. He not only obeyed the Lord, but my mother did as well. Psalm 37 became like a lighthouse, guiding a broken vessel to shore where the healing arms of Jesus awaited, and to this day, that same passage of scripture still guides my mother, though she now sails on still waters.

Throughout God's Word, we are told of countless individuals who sought the Lord's counsel and then moved according to His commands. When David was anointed king of Israel, his new position created not only opportunities to help the people of Israel but also opposition from his adversaries. The minute David's enemies heard of his fame, they came looking for him. Yet in the midst of a fiery trial, David inquired of the Lord.

Read 2 Samuel 5:17-25.

According to verse 19, what did David ask the Lord?

What was God's response?

Did David walk according to God's Word or according to his own understanding?

> **As the enemies came against David once again, what action did he take?**
>
>
> **What was God's response this time?**

Reread verse 25:

> **Then David did so, just as the LORD had commanded him, and struck down the Philistines from Geba as far as Gezer.**

Go back and underline, "<u>Then David did so, just as the LORD had commanded him.</u>"

Saul was chosen to be king over Israel. At first, he obeyed the Lord's commands for his life and assumed responsibility for his leadership role. Later on, Saul chose to disobey the Lord's directions. Instead of seeking God's counsel, Saul obtained advice from a medium.

Read 1 Chronicles 10:13:

> **So Saul died for his trespass which he committed against the LORD, because of the word of the LORD which he did not keep; and also because he asked counsel of a medium, making inquiry of it.**

Go back and underline, "<u>Because of the word of the LORD which he did not keep.</u>"

Before Saul, God used Moses to bring the children of Israel out of bondage. However, in a moment of disobedience, Moses suffered a great loss.

Read Numbers 20:8-13.

> **According to verse 8, what instructions did the Lord give Moses?**
>
>
> **How did Moses disobey the Lord's counsel?**

Look once more at verse 12:

> **But the LORD said to Moses and Aaron, "Because you have not believed Me, to treat Me as holy in the sight of the sons of Israel, therefore you shall not bring this assembly into the land which I have given them."**

Go back and underline, "<u>Because you have not believed Me.</u>" When Moses acted in complete opposition to the Lord's command, he disrespected the Lord and did not treat Him "as holy" in the sight of Israel.

> **What was the cost of Moses' rebellion?**

The New Testament account of God's command to Paul gives us a positive example. Look closely at Paul's instructions from the Lord and how he obeyed them:

> **A vision appeared to Paul in the night: a man of Macedonia was standing and appealing to him, and saying, "Come over to Macedonia and help us." When he had seen the vision, immediately we sought to go into Macedonia, concluding that God had called us to preach the gospel to them. (Acts 16:9-10)**

> **Who called Paul?**

Go back and underline in your text, "<u>immediately we sought to go</u>."

Joshua heard clearly from the Lord about how to take Jericho. Instead of debating the Lord's commands, Joshua surrendered to His will.

Read Joshua 6:6-11:

> **So Joshua the son of Nun called the priests and said to them, "Take up the ark of the covenant, and let seven priests carry seven trumpets of rams' horns before the ark of the LORD." Then he said to the people, "Go forward, and march around the city, and let the armed men go on before the ark of the LORD." And it was so, that when Joshua had spoken to the people, the seven priests carrying the seven trumpets of rams' horns before the LORD went forward and blew the trumpets; and the ark of the covenant of the LORD followed them. The armed men went before the priests who blew the trumpets, and the rear guard came after the ark, while they continued to blow the trumpets. But Joshua commanded the people, saying, "You shall not shout nor let your voice be heard nor let a word proceed out of your mouth, until the day I tell you, 'Shout!' Then you shall shout!" So he had the ark of the LORD taken around the city, circling it once; then they came into the camp and spent the night in the camp.**

Jericho was only days away from destruction. Yet in their eagerness, the children of Israel did not forge ahead with their own plans; rather, they followed the instructions of the Lord. Their obedience to God would pay off in the long run. It always does!

A pastor once stated, "One of the greatest things God will ever say to you is the last thing He said to you." Ladies, we must pay heed to God's Word. Has He pointed out a specific sin in your life that needs attention? Has He asked you to remove yourself from a particular friendship or relationship? Is He calling you to teach a class or serve in some particular area of ministry? Whatever He is asking of you, do it. God's way is always better than our own. You will never go wrong in following the Lord's instructions. Onward! The walls are coming down.

Day 3: Do Not Give Up

I was angry, tired, and hopeless. I had waited and waited on God to intervene in a particular situation I was facing. My emotions were out of control, and unbelief was assaulting my heart. Then it happened. I gave up. I had drifted to a sideline of hopelessness. However, God would not leave me in that state. He intervened and reassured my heart with His hope. I was reminded yet again that my time was not His time, and my Jericho was His responsibility. I was to trust and follow Him.

Discouragement is a visitor that knocks at the door of many hearts. It longs to move in and take up residence. And when it does, it decorates the walls of our hearts with unwanted reminders of our current situations. Over and over it floods our souls with despairing messages. If we are not careful, it will take up permanent residence in our lives.

The children of Israel were about to conquer Jericho. God was setting the stage and getting everything ready. His instructions had been given, and the Israelites were walking according to His commands.

Read Joshua 6:12-14:

> **Now Joshua rose early in the morning, and the priests took up the ark of the LORD. The seven priests carrying the seven trumpets of rams' horns before the ark of the LORD went on continually, and blew the trumpets; and the armed men went before them and the rear guard came after the ark of the LORD, while they continued to blow the trumpets. Thus the second day they marched around the city once and returned to the camp; they did so for six days.**

In looking back over your journey, can you ever recall a time where you became weary in the waiting and were tempted to quit? Or do you remember a trial that left devastation in its wake? Can you remember how God later revealed that at the point of your greatest distress, He was near with an answer?

Without realizing it, God's plan for us is often close to becoming a reality. We have no idea that God is about to move on our behalf. Yet in all truthfulness, He is. God's appointed time for our breakthroughs are often closest when the temptation for discouragement seems the greatest.

Read Acts 27:1-20.

According to verse 9, what did the sailors recognize?

According to verses 14–15, what had transpired up to this point on the journey?

At the beginning of the voyage, the storm was pounding the ship, yet the people continued to work together in good spirits. However, as time went by and the storm became worse, hopelessness set in.

Read verse 20 once more:

> **Since neither sun nor stars appeared for many days, and no small storm was assailing us, from then on all hope of our being saved was gradually abandoned.**

> **According to verse 20, what circumstances had led to their hopelessness?**

Go back and underline, "<u>from then on all hope of our being saved was gradually abandoned.</u>"

> **Have you ever abandoned something that at one time was very special to your life? What was the result?**

The people on board the ship with Paul were greatly distressed. They had abandoned hope. Though they did not know it, a miracle was on the way.

Read Acts 27:20-44.

> **According to verses 21–26, what message of hope did Paul not only receive but convey to the people on the ship?**
>
> **What was the basis for this encouraging message?**
>
> **Take a few moments to write out verse 25:**
>
> **Reread verse 27. What had the sailors discovered around midnight?**
>
> **According to verse 29, what did they fear?**
>
> **What actions did some of the sailors take out of fear (v. 30)?**

> ## Who stopped them from escaping?

Attached to the side of the ship was an escape boat. Even though Paul had communicated the message from the Lord about their safe arrival, some of the sailors allowed fear to control them. Instead of trusting in what the Lord had spoken, they attempted to flee the situation.

Escape boats: They are everywhere. If a marriage gets too hard, people flee. If a job becomes too much, people quit. If a prayer is not answered in what they consider to be a timely manner, they stop praying. It is often easier to jump on an escape boat than to stick with what God has called us to do. Yet in the long run, we will miss His best if we attempt to run instead of staying His course.

Look once more at Paul's declaration to those who were trying to escape: Paul said to the centurion and to the soldiers, "Unless these men remain in the ship, you yourselves cannot be saved."

Go back and underline, "<u>Unless these men remain in the ship</u>." Listen, there will always be moments of temptation where we wish to escape from something that is too hard. Yet if we cave into fear's cry and run, we may miss the miracle God is waiting to give us.

Read verse 32 once more:

Then the soldiers cut away the ropes of the ship's boat and let it fall away.

What action did the soldiers take in regard to the escape boat? They cut away the ropes. In other words, in moving forward, that particular avenue of escape would no longer be an option.

Listen, ladies: we all have a shoreline awaiting us. Our journey is going somewhere, and even though the horizon may look dark and bleak, we must remember that it is God who superintends our journey.

A few years ago, I read a story about a young lady who inspired my heart. I want to conclude with this story today.

Florence May Chadwick, age twenty-four, attempted to swim twenty-three miles across the Catalina Channel. After swimming fifteen hours and fifty-five minutes in an ice-cold ocean surrounded by dense fog, she began to doubt her ability to make it. With her mom in the boat encouraging her to continue, she persisted in her swim. Then, with only a half mile to go, she gave up.

Two months later, this same young lady decided to try again, and even though she faced the same dense fog as she had before, she kept a mental image of the shoreline in her mind and made it. The difference the second time around was her focus.

Chadwick could not change the circumstances that surrounded her on either day; however, she did change the way she looked at them. The end result of her second attempt was that she reached her destination.

At a news conference, after Chadwick's first attempt to swim the Catalina Channel, she was recorded as saying, "All I could see was the fog. I think if I could have seen the shore, I would have made it." Does this resonate with you?

The race that is set before us will never be wasted, nor is our faith, hope, and belief. Do not give up on what God has said. Your miracle may be just around the corner. Despite the fog that is in your way, keep pressing on, and know with certainty your shoreline awaits.

Let us not lose heart in doing good, for in due time we will reap if we do not grow weary. (Galatians 6:9)

Day 4: I Do Not See Anything Happening

The seventh day had finally come! The children of Israel awoke early to face one of the most important days of their lives. The walls were just hours away from collapsing. However, it would not be an instant dissolution. The Israelites would march around the wall seven times in one day before the Lord would bring the walls down.

Read Joshua 6:15:

> **Then on the seventh day they rose early at the dawning of the day and marched around the city in the same manner seven times; only on that day they marched around the city seven times.**

I can only imagine their faces on this special day as they proceeded to walk around the city.

For just a moment, travel back with me in your mind to when the Israelites were encircling Jericho. Pretend we are watching them from afar. Join me in cheering them on as they march seven times around the wall. *Note: We already know the ending. So cheer really loud. Here they go.*

Children of Israel's Jericho

> **Round one: (They look inspired) We cheer, "Keep marching."**
>
> **Rounds two and three: (They are hopeful) We cheer, "Keep marching."**
>
> **Rounds four and five: (They look tired) We cheer, "Keep marching."**
>
> **Round six: (They are praying) We cheer, "Keep marching."**
>
> **Round seven: Victory!**

Many of us face a similar battle of faith today. We are enthusiastic about moving forward at the onset of God's promise. Yet as time drags on and we do not see anything happening, we become discouraged.

> **What Jericho are you facing?**

Now, let us revisit a different Jericho. I want you to pretend a group of ladies are watching you from afar as you march around your own personal Jericho. I am one of those individuals cheering you on. Ready? Here we go.

Your Own Jericho

> **Round one: (You look encouraged) "Keep marching."**
>
> **Rounds two and three: (You seem tired) "Keep marching."**
>
> **Round four: (Keep your focus upward) "Keep marching."**

Round five: (You are almost there) "Keep marching."

Round six: (You have stopped. What's wrong? Get back up! God is intervening) "Keep marching."

Round seven: Walls fall.

Now, let us do one last exercise. I want to invite you to a Jericho of my own—one I most recently lived out. I want you to watch from afar, but instead of cheering, I want you to listen to God's cheers.

My Jericho

Round one: (I heard from the Lord, and it is a done deal) He says, "Keep marching."

Round two: (Months have passed, Lord, and nothing is happening. I still believe) He says, "Keep marching."

Round three: (I may have heard wrong, Lord. Maybe I misread what You were saying) He says, "Keep marching."

Round four: (I am tired, Lord. I am so tired) He says, "Keep marching."

Round five: (Unbelief has entered) He says, "Keep marching."

Round six: (I see nothing matching what You have spoken) He says, "Keep marching."

Round seven: "My child, here is your miracle. Take it."

We must always remember to move forward with God in spite of our circumstances and emotions. For if we stop, sit down, and give up, we may miss His best.

I remember listening intently to my friend express grief over a trial her husband was facing. He was called into the ministry; however, instead of pastoring a church, he found himself working a secular job. Year after year passed, and nothing seemed to materialize. Finally, in the couple's seventh year of waiting, the Lord placed the gentleman in a wonderful ministry position.

During his job interview with the church, he said the following: "As I was pushing shopping carts in the rain, I asked God a question: *Is this it, Lord? Is this where I am supposed to be for the rest of my life?*" Certainly, nothing was wrong with the job in which he was engaged. He was quite thankful to be employed. The heart of the matter was this: He was called to preach, and in God's time, that vision was fulfilled.

Hopelessness often comes when we trust in our limited vision more than we do in Jesus. Though the children of Israel could not see anything happening, they believed God and kept marching. We must pray for God to open our eyes when we cannot see so that with His help, we can conquer our Jericho.

Read 2 Kings 6:8-17.

Elisha sent word to the king of Israel to be careful, for an ambush had been set up for him. Yet, when the king of Aram found out that Elisha was telling the king of Israel his plans, he became furious.

Reread verses 11–14.

> **What actions did King Aram take? Record them in order from verse 14.**

Look again at verse 15:

> **Now when the attendant of the man of God had risen early and gone out, behold, an army with horses and chariots was circling the city. And his servant said to him, "Alas, my master! What shall we do?"**

What did Elisha's attendant see? Go back and circle, "an army with horses and chariots."

Where were they located? Go back and underline, "circling the city."

> **At this point, what else did the servant see?**
>
> **What question did the servant ask Elisha (v. 15)?**

Elisha's first response to his servant's fear was a three-word message: "Do not fear."

> **According to verse 16, what was his second message of hope?**

Let us review verse 17:

> **Then Elisha prayed and said, "O Lord, I pray, open his eyes that he may see." And the Lord opened the servant's eyes and he saw; and behold, the mountain was full of horses and chariots of fire all around Elisha.**

> **Why did Elisha ask the Lord to open the eyes of his servant?**
>
> **What did the servant observe when God granted Elisha's request?**

At the beginning of the crisis, Elisha's servant saw only the enemies. However, when God opened his eyes, he witnessed numerous soldiers in battle array, waiting to advance against Israel's adversaries.

Listen, friend, you may not be able to see anything happening with regard to your situation, but let me be clear: God is at work. Ask Him to open your eyes to see clearly what He is doing in and through the situation you are facing.

No matter what or how many times God asks you to do something, do it. Whether it is seven days, seven months, or seven years, keep moving forward with Him. "Keep marching!"

Day 5: The Walls Come Down

What an incredible journey this has been for all of us. For the past seven weeks, we have immersed ourselves in the Word of God, gleaning the riches of His wisdom for our journey here. We have both wept and worshipped, while studying the many lessons God has for us in this study. In addition, we have been awed by God's love, His faithfulness, His provision, and His guidance for the children of Israel. What an amazing Savior we have!

It was a long journey for the Israelites. Yet here they were eager to see the walls come down. It was the fulfillment of a miraculous promise. Yesterday, we read about the children of Israel marching around Jericho seven times. Let us finish by reading Joshua 6:16-27:

> **At the seventh time, when the priests blew the trumpets, Joshua said to the people, "Shout! For the LORD has given you the city. The city shall be under the ban, it and all that is in it belongs to the LORD; only Rahab the harlot and all who are with her in the house shall live, because she hid the messengers whom we sent. But as for you, only keep yourselves from the things under the ban, so that you do not covet them and take some of the things under the ban, and make the camp of Israel accursed and bring trouble on it. But all the silver and gold and articles of bronze and iron are holy to the LORD; they shall go into the treasury of the LORD." So the people shouted, and priests blew the trumpets; and when the people heard the sound of the trumpet, the people shouted with a great shout and the wall fell down flat, so that the people went up into the city, every man straight ahead, and they took the city. They utterly destroyed everything in the city, both man and woman, young and old, and ox and sheep and donkey, with the edge of the sword. Joshua said to the two men who had spied out the land, "Go into the harlot's house and bring the woman and all she has out of there, as you have sworn to her." So the young men who were spies went in and brought out Rahab and her father and her mother and her brothers and all she had; they also brought out all her relatives and placed them outside the camp of Israel. They burned the city with fire, and all that was in it. Only the silver and gold, and articles of bronze and iron, they put into the treasury of the house of the LORD. However, Rahab the harlot and her father's household and all she had, Joshua spared; and she has lived in the midst of Israel to this day, for she hid the messengers whom Joshua sent to spy out Jericho. Then Joshua made them take an oath at that time, saying, "Cursed before the LORD is the man who rises up and builds this city Jericho; with the loss of his firstborn he shall lay its foundation, and with the loss of his youngest son he shall set up its gates." So the LORD was with Joshua, and his fame was in all the land.**

> **According to verse 20, what had the Israelites accomplished?**

Notice the end of verse 20: "And they took the city." God had given His promise, His instructions, and His guidance. Now, He had given the children of Israel His victory. Look at Joshua 5:13-15 once more:

> **Now it came about when Joshua was by Jericho, that he lifted up his eyes and looked, and behold, a man was standing opposite him with his sword drawn in his hand, and Joshua went to him and said to him, "Are you for us or for our adversaries?" He said, "No; rather I indeed come now as captain of the host of the LORD." And Joshua fell on his face to the earth, and bowed down, and said to him, "What has my lord to say to his servant?" The captain of the LORD's host said to Joshua, "Remove your sandals from your feet, for the place where you are standing is holy." And Joshua did so.**

In Joshua 5, as Joshua gazed at Jericho, he might very well have felt some fear. Yet, God knows all things. He sees when we struggle, when we fear, and when we wonder how in the world those walls are going to come down. Once again (for this is such an important reminder), why did Christ come with a drawn sword? He wanted to remind a fearful Joshua that He was in charge of Jericho, of the Israelites, and of their journey. He wanted Joshua to trust Him and to obey Him. My sister, He wants the same for you today.

As a single mom rearing my children, I can look back at the many times fear nearly paralyzed me. With certainty, I can say today that God was faithful through every anxious moment and performed more miracles than I can list. He never once abandoned Randy and Mandy, my children, nor did He ever leave me. He walked with us through the fires and trials of life, intervening as only He could, providing in ways I could have never imagined, and drawing a mother and her two children to His side.

I wish I could write here the many prayers I prayed for my children, as well as the many answers the Lord gave. One has most recently been answered. As I was penning this last day of this study, my son, Randy, was saved. This past Sunday, he obeyed God's command to be baptized. As I sat in the pew of the church and watched the preacher bring my son up out of the water, I shouted with joy, *Amen!* Moms, God hears your prayers for your children.

Obedience always opens the door for blessings. When we obey the commands of Christ, He will do more than you and I ever thought possible. Keep praying for your children, keep living for Jesus, and keep moving forward with Him—but move forward in obedience. Dr. Charles Stanley states, "Obey God and leave all the consequences up to Him."[19]

Remember and never forget God sees you, He loves you, and He will guide you and your children throughout your journey. Those Jerichos, those walls, and all that you will ever face are under the Lord's authority and watchful eye, and so are you and your children. Rest in this truth: God is the One over your journey, so keep moving forward with Him, trusting in Him every step of the way, for He will always be faithful to you and to yours.

To pass on to you the many lessons the Lord has entrusted to me has been a joy. My prayers are with you, and my cheers are for you. Moms, through Christ, you can do this. You are adored by our Savior. Onward!

---

19 Charles Stanley is known for saying this throughout his lifetime.

Notes

Additional Notes for Weekly Lessons

Afterword

Thank you for your hard work during this seven-week Bible study. I am so proud of you! Always remember, sweet mom, God sees you and your children, and He promises to never leave nor forsake His own. Follow Him, trust Him, obey Him, and know with certainty you have value and you have purpose! God will guide you, protect you, and provide for you. Be strong and courageous, sister—for God loves you and is always working on your behalf! He will be faithful to you and to yours.

Explore Additional Resources at
InnovoPublishing.com

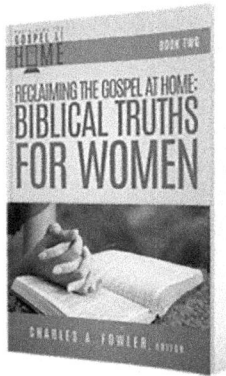

Biblical Truths for Women
by Charles Fowler

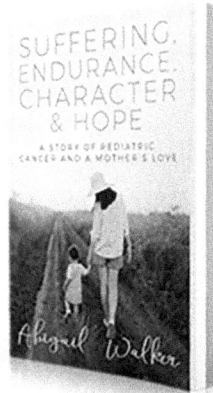

Suffering, Endurance,
Character & Hope
by Abigail Walker

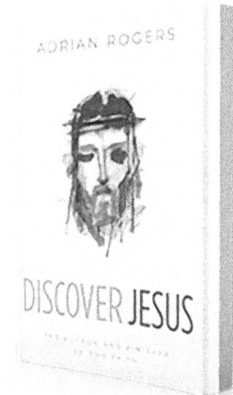

Discover Jesus
by Adrian Rogers

Good Morning, Lord
by Adrian Rogers

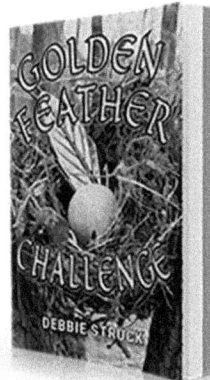

Golden Feather Challenge
by Debbie Struck

His Story
by Adrian Rogers

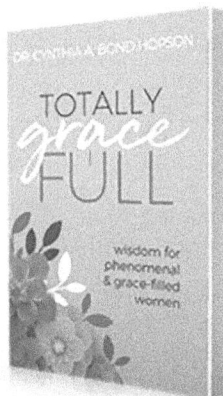

Totall Grace-FULL
by Cynthia Hopson

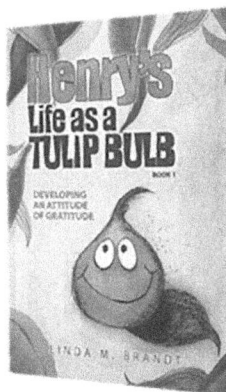

Henry's Life as a Tulip Bulb
by Linda Brandt

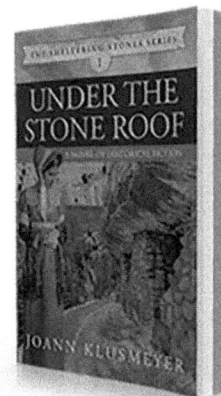

Under the Stone Roof
by Joann Klusmeyer

www.ingramcontent.com/pod-product-compliance
Lightning Source LLC
Chambersburg PA
CBHW080533090426
42733CB00015B/2577